THE ACTOR'S WAYS AND MEANS

THE ROCKEFELLER FOUNDATION LECTURES
DEPARTMENT OF DRAMA
UNIVERSITY OF BRISTOL, 1952-53

KING LEAR

Shakespeare Memorial Theatre, Stratford-on-Avon, 1953

MICHAEL REDGRAVE

THE ACTOR'S
WAYS AND MEANS

THEATRE ARTS BOOKS

NEW YORK

FIRST PUBLISHED 1953
REPRINTED 1954, 1956, 1961

PUBLISHED BY
THEATRE ARTS BOOKS
333 SIXTH AVENUE, NEW YORK 14
PRINTED IN GREAT BRITAIN
BY MORRISON & GIBB LTD., EDINBURGH

TO MY MOTHER

MARGARET SCUDAMORE

Foreword

ONE of the first considerations of the speaker is the nature of his audience. The text of this book is that of the Rockefeller Foundation Lectures which I was asked to deliver in the Department of Drama at Bristol University during the session of 1952-53. The first of the lectures, it was suggested, should be a public one, to a mixed audience of over a thousand: first Drama Department students, then students of the University, pupils of the Bristol Old Vic School, members of the Bristol Old Vic Theatre Company and the Bristol general public. To the following three lectures the public was not admitted. This promised to work out quite well, for it permitted me in the first lecture to approach my subject in a general way, but I was aware even then that my questions were more plentiful than my answers and that those answers were not so much supplied as suggested.

A real complication was that it is a condition of the lectureship that the lectures should eventually be published. This meant that my remarks would reach a far different if not a much larger audience, and that this audience would include not only my fellow-actors but also some of the dramatic critics, whose job it is to set some kind of seal on our performances. What a player actually does on the stage—what he projects to the audience—is of more importance than what he may think ought to be done. This thought frequently halted my pen and has delayed revision for publication.

The revision, however, is not extensive. What chiefly caused my pen to lag was the thought that since the actor's conception of his powers and functions are continually in an O'Casey-like 'state of chassis' I might well be thinking quite differently about my subject in six months' time. At the moment of writing I do not do so, but as I warned the first audience to the lectures I cannot regard these talks as anything but an interim statement. I have pruned here and there, amplified where I thought my meaning obscure and relegated certain digressions to the notes at the end.

I would like to thank the Bristol University Drama Department, and in particular Mr. Glynne Wickham and Professor Kitto, for their help, encouragement and hospitality; also my friend Professor Sir Dennis Robertson for his help in correction of my syntax and my proofs.

CONTENTS

LIST OF ILLUSTRATIONS

I

Cause and Effect

. . . once we have become conscious in any degree of the technical demands which the artist has to meet, whether self-consciously or unconsciously, then we must go the whole hog. . . . If we are committed to critical sophistication we must go all the way. . . . (^{1})

I HAVE been quoting from a modern critic of the novel. I might wish that I also could go so far, or even tell you half as much about acting. I might also wish to 'go the whole hog'. But it is best to admit that even if I did, I would find it beyond me. In any case, it is not my wish. My mind may like to enquire, but its enquiries take, as a rule, a discursive form. Analysis does not come easily to me. 'Character' I can only apprehend—rashly or cautiously; sometimes—as when the character has affinities with my own—some traits of my own—swiftly and successfully; sometimes not at all. My acquaintance with the theory of acting, as theory, is a prolonged liaison, little or nothing more. In short, I think it is permitted to the actor, as to other artists, to add up many or most of the figures of his professional ledger and yet be allowed not to attempt to make out the final sum. 'The players will tell all,' says Hamlet. This player, even if he knew, would not tell. Not all. Therefore you are unlikely to take away from these lectures, in sum, anything but a small total: a personal, temporary valuation, something that can at best only be called an attitude. If this personal attitude contains any kind of stimulus, one way or another, so much the better.

The late Sir Desmond MacCarthy, reviewing a book on Elizabethan acting, referred to the difference—a difference of which he said he had been aware all his life—'between those who love the theatre and those who prefer "literary experience".' Now there is much truth in the belief that in the theatre, as in the study, the poet's words are all that count. I want to leave that consideration to the last of these talks, for it is not, as Sir Desmond MacCarthy emphatically pointed out, the whole truth. He goes on: 'Vitally important as the poet's words are—or for that matter, his ideas—in the theatre something else also counts: namely, the actor's power to make us feel as if he really was the man he impersonates. It is not everything or "all" that we should exclaim, "How perfectly he spoke that speech!" With what nicety of intonation he marked its changing meanings! The summit of the actor's art is also to make us forget that he is an actor; only then do we share intimately the experience of his character's creator.' (2)

Why is there the difference which Sir Desmond MacCarthy points out? Why do some take the high road and some take the low road? Why do some of our best authors never write for the theatre? It is perhaps in our country, which produced the greatest dramatic poet that the world has ever known, that this difference —between those who love the theatre and those who much prefer 'literary experience'—is most marked, and it is notable that except for the isolated and for the most part unproduced plays of some of our great poets—Keats, Byron, Shelley and Tennyson— the great literary figures have for some time only attempted what is at best a flirtation with the theatre. (There are, of course, honourable exceptions to this—Galsworthy, Eliot, Priestley, Morgan and others.) I cannot explain why this is so. I can only point out that it is, and that the phenomenon has at the present moment become very marked. As Mr. Richard Findlater in a recent book(3) has pointed out, in France we find the great intellectuals such as Gide, Cocteau, Claudel and Bernanos, together with the great contemporary novelists such as Sartre, Mauriac, Roger Martin du Gard and Jules Supervielle producing a number of plays. Where, Mr. Findlater most pertinently asked, are the plays, say, of Graham Greene,(4) George Orwell, Rex Warner, E. M. Forster, Edith Sitwell, Percy Wyndham Lewis, Cecil Day Lewis, Harold Nicolson, Evelyn Waugh, Herbert Read, Elizabeth Bowen and Joyce Cary?

I am not blaming our modern writers. I am simply, like Mr. Findlater, asking a question, and suggesting that since all these authors represent a considerable body of opinion—or rather that through their works they express much of the feeling of the time —there is indeed a very strange and uneven relationship between the English intellectual and English theatrical way of life.

How far is the actor to blame for this?

At the dividing of the two paths, the high road and the low road, welcoming those who love the theatre and alarming those who prefer literary experience, stands the professional actor. The effulgent and repulsive, brilliant, banal, acclaimed and despised actor; the actor, with his exaggerations, his vanities, his overweening self-importance or unworthy intellect, seems to stand on the dividing line between the creative writer and the theatre public.

There he is, familiar and yet alarming, like a scarecrow. There can be no doubt that to many he represents much of what is vulgar and insincere. Hamlet himself lets us see how he is at once loved and hated. The ambivalence persists today. There are ten thousand instances of how the actor will betray his art, his author or himself.

Yet hear what the late Jean Giraudoux says of him: 'L'acteur n'est pas seulement interprète, il est un inspirateur . . . et le grand acteur: un grand inspirateur.'(5)

It would be not unfair to say that there are, roughly speaking, two kinds of actor: those who primarily play for effect and those who, whether by instinct or method, seek for cause before making their effect. But even this cannot be elevated into a dictum, for those who play primarily for effect—or as we say in the theatre, 'from outside'—are by no means unaware that they must indicate, and to some extent feel, the cause or motivation which should precede that bid for effect. Similarly, those artists who try to discover primarily the truth of a character are also usually aware to some extent of the effect they are creating.

The best title on any thesis on acting was used by Diderot in his *Paradox sur le comédien*. Acting is indeed a paradox. I am no Diderot, no little Lessing, no baby Bertold Brecht. I shall not attempt to resolve the paradox. I shall not elevate any theory of my own into a rule. My aim is only to show this paradox as I see it.

The first thing we notice is that our very terms of reference, our vocabulary, are not only suspiciously but maddeningly vague. Their very vagueness indicates the peril of the paradox. In France a distinction has been drawn and pointed by, among others, the late Louis Jouvet between the words *acteur* and *comédien*. In round terms, to Jouvet, the *acteur* represents the 'personality actor,' the man who can be relied on to go on and give a performance which may help the play to unfold its story, but who in so doing moulds a character in lines set by his own. The *comédien* (which of course has nothing whatever to do with a comedian or comic actor) is the actor who, by sinking his own personality or by, as it were, translating or in some cases exceeding it, brings, according to Jouvet, something of the same creative process to bear on his part as the author has brought to the creation of the character.

Our terms, as I said, are vague. For instance, we all think we know what it means, yet few can agree on the meaning of the popular phrase 'ham'. If we were to talk of a classical actor it would be supposed that we mean an actor who appears mainly in Shakespeare and other 'classics'. By 'romantic actor' we would seem to mean the actor who plays lovers. By 'character actor' we generally mean a supporting actor who either undertakes to disguise himself or who substitutes a well-known personality for the author's character. We seldom think of the actors of Richard III, or King Claudius, or Richard II, or Joseph Surface as giving character performances.

It is not difficult to see the reason for this confusion. Nowadays every branch and aspect of acting may to some extent overlap others. It is certainly a preferable state of affairs to the old stock-company categories of 'leading-man,' 'leading-woman,' 'heavy,' 'walking-gentleman' and so forth. It is better than considering, as the French used to say, whether a part were 'dans son emploi.'

But it means that our understanding of the art or craft of acting (there again, which do *you* say: *art or craft?*) remains largely a *mystique*. Even so astute a practitioner as Jouvet[6] can admit to being impressed by the mysterious mathematics of the theatre. Why should a successful play, drawing, let us say, one hundred thousand people for one hundred performances draw approximately one thousand only each night? Why do not four thousand people besiege the box-office on any one night? No doubt your sense of

ORLANDO

in *As You Like It*
with Edith Evans
Old Vic, 1937

Angus McBean

ANTONY

in *Antony and Cleopatra*
with Peggy Ashcroft
Shakespeare Memorial
Theatre, Stratford-on-
Avon, 1953

Angus McBean

BOLINGBROKE

in *Richard II,* with
Leon Quartermaine
Queen's Theatre, 1937

Houston Rogers

RICHARD II

Shakespeare Memorial
Theatre, Stratford-on-
Avon, 1951

Angus McBean

the laws of chance can answer that. But can you say why one member of an audience can so affect spectators near him that unless or until he is won over by the play and the acting their sympathies are not fully engaged? Why can one small-part actor, bodily present on the stage but with his thoughts elsewhere, rob a scene of its full effect, nullify it even, when to all appearances he is 'acting'? Jouvet tells us that in both cases the 'magnetic field' is disturbed, and most actors would swallow that term since it lends a kind of dignity to phenomena with which we are all too well acquainted and all too unable to explain.

The dicta of great actors, like those of other men, have to be interpreted in the light of their personalities and times. They range from the simple to the profound and back to the superficial, and are scarcely less sensible or more silly than the pronouncements of other public figures.

It is when you come to put them into practice that the trouble begins. Irving's 'Speak clearly! Speak clearly and be human' makes good sense, but unfortunately everyone imagines he is speaking clearly enough, and to be told to speak still more clearly can produce artificiality and at once we seem to be less 'human'. Rossi's requirements for the tragic actor, 'Voice, voice and then —more voice,' coming from a notable Othello, might suggest that every tragic actor should be able to roar like a bull. What he meant was that within the limits of a big voice there should be another voice and then still other voices. Bull-like voices tend to go with bull-like figures, and we also remember that there have been great actors of insignificant physique and very limited vocal range, and then where are we?

Listen for a moment to some words of Sarah Bernhardt: 'You must always think of your pleasure. It is up to you to be demanding, severe, a person of taste.' She is talking to the students of the Conservatoire. Unamiable sentiments, you may think, excellent advice perhaps; but . . . for students? 'You only really begin to act,' I have heard our greatest native actress say, 'when you leave off trying.' But some have to try much longer than others, and the moment to leave off trying dictates itself and cannot be chosen.

With what relief do actors turn to the only half-humorous sayings of the tried and trusty 'pro'. 'Whenever an actress tells

me she can't quite *feel* something,' said the actor-author-producer,
'I tell her, "Learn yer words, dear, and you'll *feel* it all right".' He
had been probing me about Stanislavski, whose *My Life in Art* I
had thoughtlessly left lying about my dressing-room. 'Wasn't
that that little Russian company?' he asked, 'who went away to
the country to rehearse for two years, and then weren't ready to
open?' I have never met any actor or actress who did not glow
with pleasure, as I do, at the reply of the actress to the producer
who told her during rehearsals, 'That's very good, it's coming
nicely.' 'What do you mean, "coming"? This is *IT*!' How en-
dearing is the simplicity of Réjane's answer to one who asked her
how she always managed to cry real tears on the stage, 'C'est mon
métier!' Joseph Jefferson's comment on the great Coquelin con-
troversy ('Should an Actor feel?') could hardly be more charmingly
and lucidly phrased: 'For myself,' said Jefferson, 'I know that I act
best when my head is cool and my heart is warm.' But how does
an actor put it into practice?

What, too, does an actor learn from the words of the greatest
actor-dramatist of them all? Have you ever noticed that all the
First Player says in reply to Hamlet's advice on acting is, '*I warrant
your Honour*' and '*I hope we have reformed that indifferently with us*'?
The Players may have been on a foreign tour but the replies are
worthy of the Foreign Office. It is easy to say that in the torrent
tempest and whirlwind of passion should be acquired and begot
a temperance to give it smoothness—but—how is it done? How
certain can you be that 'your own discretion' is a good tutor? The
Advice to the Players is, I think, a piece of 'pure theatre,' like the
'Rogue and Peasant-Slave' soliloquy which starts with Hamlet
sharing Polonius' amazement that a man should weep in a fiction
and a dream of passion, and goes on to show Hamlet unpack his
heart with words and fall a-cursing like a very drab, in frustrated
passion. There is a lesson here for us. For the *Advice to the Players*
is Diderot's paradox dramatised, the paradox which Jacques Copeau
dramatised in his *L'Illusion*, a play written especially for and about
his company—his *Impromptu de Versailles* for the *Compagnie des
Quinze*. It is the paradox which obsessed Pirandello, who realised
that the paradox of the player is the paradox of human life. The
Advice to the Players in *Hamlet* is a conjuring trick raised to a work

of art. And like a conjuring trick it tells us nothing. For practical information we might as well turn to the causeries of some forgotten actor.

And if we do turn to these we find, most notably, a strong distrust of method and analysis in acting. Intelligence or intellect are tabu. We English at any rate seem to think, like Trinculo, that we 'know what belongs to a frippery.'

Even Fanny Kemble, who was what might be called a 'highbrow' actress, with at least a glint of a blue stocking peeping from under her tuppence-coloured petticoat, declared that 'greater intellectual cultivation and a purer and more elevated taste, are unfavourable to the existence of the true theatrical spirit.'

Here, indeed, is a common crux of theatrical as well as æsthetic opinion. It is also an important one. While suggesting to you that for the moment you should note it and ask yourselves, if you have not already done so, what you think is the answer, I propose to leave consideration of it to those occasions which I have cautiously titled 'Instinct and Method'.

By one of those strange chances which happen when we are especially seeking one thing and we stumble on something else, I opened, as I prepared these lectures, a book by William Archer: criticisms of our theatre in the nineties. I had, I thought, glanced at it often before. What I did not know was that some previous owner, on a day in 1924, had cut out and folded up in it *The Times* obituary of Eleonora Duse, together with an appreciation of the actress by *The Times* critic of that time, A. B. Walkley. I quote it, neither in praise nor in condemnation of Walkley. It is a question of which way you look at it. Walkley writes of Duse:

It is true that she was no mere mime. Just as there are writers who can faithfully reproduce every style under the sun, but have no style of their own, so there are actors—'Protean' they used to be called—who pride themselves on concealing their individuality under innumerable disguises. The fact is, they have no individuality to conceal. Such vogue as still survives for your Protean actor rests upon the fallacy, now become flyblown, that art is imitation.

2

Acting can imitate only external things, gestures, accents and looks. What makes it an art is the spirit that informs it, and is expressed through it. When the actor attempts to express what is not in his own spirit he ceases to be an artist, and becomes (what, indeed, the Greeks called him) a hypocrite—he presents effects divorced from causes. (7)

But who are, in fact, 'the writers who can reproduce every style under the sun,' but 'who have no style of their own'? There are none. The best parodists, like Beerbohm, have also their own unmistakable style. Who, and this is Walkley's analogy, are the 'Protean' actors who attempt the same feat? The same impossible feat? Walkley is right when he says that acting can imitate—and I am assuming that the operative word is *imitate*—'only external things, gestures, accents, and looks'. When he deduces that 'when the actor attempts to express what is not in his own spirit' and so on, I think he falls short. For the actor, unless we are talking of the miscast repertory actor, makes no such attempt (and in an obituary of such an actress as Duse we are not talking in terms of 'repertory' acting). The actor who has won for himself some say and choice in his parts does not usually attempt 'to express what is not in his own spirit.'

Yet that spirit may not be there in such surplus that success is guaranteed, as it can be with some actors in some roles. Irving may fail on the first nights of Lear and of Romeo, as he is said to have done. But the idea that Irving had nothing of Lear, less than nothing of Romeo in his make-up is inconceivable, for the essence of both these characters should lie within the compass of all actors whom Walkley contemptuously calls 'Protean'. That he was perhaps neither the perfect Lear nor the ideal Romeo only serves my point; a point which is best expressed by Henry James in his essay on Coquelin. James gives the best and last word on what I would call classic as opposed to romantic acting. (Let me make myself quite clear on this point, by classic I mean Walkley's despised Protean actor, by romantic I mean the process whereby an actor translates each role into his own personality. I am aware that the definitions are not complete. I suggest that you try to work out your own.) Here is Henry James, in full flood of praise over the actor he most admired: Coquelin, then about to embark on an American tour:

To enjoy the refinement of his acting, however, the ear must be as open as the eye, must even be beforehand with it; and if that of the American spectator in general learns, or even shows an aptitude for learning, the lesson conveyed in his finest creations, the lesson that acting is an art, and that the application of an art is style, and that style is expression and that expression is the salt of life, the gain will have been something more than the sensation of the moment; it will be a new wisdom(8).

How different in intention is this to Walkley's next two lines on the great Italian actress:

Duse, an absolute artist if ever there was one, expressed herself, her own soul, and the beauty of her acting lay in her expression.

Just so. And the beauty of Coquelin's art also lay in its expression. Sometimes expression can be comparatively small in range, even introvert, and yet universal: such is the expression of a Chardin and of a Proust. Acting, too, can be introvert or extravert. Expression again can have the wide canvas of a Rubens or a Chaucer, or like Blake it can embrace the world of now and the world to come and still remain a personal thing.

But does this distinction matter much? I think not. Expression is all that matters. And I wish to make this point especially clear because, having indicated where my sympathies as an actor lie, I still believe that some of the most exquisite and enduring work —though I should say *memorable*, for the actor's work in fact does not *endure*—is made by actors and actresses who are far from 'Protean', who are what we call 'personality actors'. I cannot repeat too forcibly that these actors often provide summits of entertainment. Chaplin, to my mind, has only two characters: the tramp, and the obverse, the dandy Verdoux or the Great Dictator. Garbo never seems to have attempted to characterise beyond a change of mood. Marie Tempest was for all waters, but she made her own wind and weather. I worship them all three.

But you will see what I am aiming at. Perhaps Walkley, from another pitch, was aiming at the same mark. There are 'personality' actors and the rest—the 'Proteans' as Walkley calls them.

'Endurability' . . .? It is a proud claim of dramatic critics that it is in their paragraphs or volumes that we actors live again. It is not so. It is they, the critics, who live again, attended by our perhaps vivid but now supernumerary ghosts. The claim is that in a moment of fine writing the critic has distilled an 'amber' in which we, the actors, are forever preserved. Would it were so! Sometimes we see the shimmer of a wing, the shape of a leg, the flash of an eye. But the limbs are those of a corpse. Some of the ingredients of a great performance are indicated, but not the excitement, not the personality, not the moment. These you can suggest, but nothing is less perdurable than these. They cannot be preserved nor recreated. What is preserved in dramatic criticism is not the performance seen by the critic but his own sensitivity.(9) I say this for only one purpose. I am not here to air my views on dramatic criticism but to talk about acting, and if what I have just said has any truth in it, and if, as we so often say, a play is only really a play the moment it is performed before an audience and—a corollary seldom noted—not a play afterwards until it is being performed again—it lays a great responsibility on the actor to make that moment magic. He must share the exultation or the conviction which makes Antony exclaim:

> the nobleness of life
> Is to do thus . . .

I will say no more of the relationship between actors and critics than this. Instinctively every artist resents criticism. We have only to think of the diatribes of Pope, the sting of Whistler's attacks, the stories of Garrick's surreptitious replies to his critics which he printed under a pseudonym, Irving's secret ownership of a theatrical magazine containing views not unfavourable to himself, Benjamin Britten's recent outcry that music criticism should only be written by practising musicians. . . .

What the artist creates, he creates in a spirit which is a spirit of love. The best criticism is informed with the same spirit. Certainly the critics whose work endures were and are imbued with the same spirit. Love can occasionally be severe in its resentment of some failing in the loved one. (Look at Hazlitt's review on Mrs. Siddons' return to the stage.) It can be savage, as Shaw knew how to be savage. It can be loving and yet frivolous and spiteful, as James Agate knew how to be. Yet who can doubt that Hazlitt, Shaw and Agate loved the theatre? The conditions in which critics work are harder than is generally supposed. I could wish they could be given more time, more space, less to do and more room in which to do it. I could also wish that the written history of our theatre were not a history of first nights.

What is the true, full function of the actor? How far does he fulfil that function in our modern theatre? How far do the conditions of the modern theatre frustrate him from fulfilling that function? How far does the actor himself frustrate the theatre's function? Where does the actor stand in relation to the author, the producer, the public? What of dramatic tradition? What, especially, are the actor's obligations—or, if you prefer it, duties —towards himself. What, in fact, are the causes and effects?

I am not going to try to answer all these questions at once. I shall count myself lucky if I answer even a few of them. The general title of these lectures, 'Ways and Means', suggests to me some kind of day-to-day or month-to-month account, and the first thing that has to be said is that this is more or less the way in which actors in this country at this time have to live and work and have their being. It has always been the way they have had to work.

It must be, I think, in the circumstances in which you work and study here, easy to forget occasionally that outside these walls, theatrically speaking, is a jungle. A very fascinating jungle it can be and by no means impenetrable, alive not only with every sort of danger, but, at the most unexpected turn, time or place, vibrant with rich and unexpected beauties.

I am not going to bore you with a long account of all the dangers of this strange forest. They have been written about and talked about for years.(10) But before any consideration of the actor's functions, social or æsthetic, can be made, it is necessary to remind you—for it can scarcely be said too often—that he lives a hard and dangerous life. Occasionally it is brimful of excitement and opportunity, but in many cases it is a lonely and frustrated one, where he remains hidden, unobserved, starving even, with little hope of rescue. It is no wonder, therefore, that the actor should occasionally fail the theatre, fail the art inside him, fail, therefore, himself.

Some of you may be thinking it obtuse and impolite of me, now, as your guest, to remind you here of such well-known facts. You know, as well as I, that some kind of talent for acting is not in itself enough. You also would be prepared to say that to be an actor needs more than talent, more even than what is called a vocation. I welcome such an institution as a Department of Drama, such as we have here. But at least so far as the prospective actors among you are concerned, I have to ask you, however rude or embarrassing it may seem: what about this jungle? This beautiful and treacherous jungle?

I will not ask you to remember the names of many who made their paths and their clearings: the names of the early Ibsen actresses, such as Elizabeth Robins and Janet Achurch, names nearly forgotten now; the name of Miss Horniman of Manchester, which still lives, and the more recent name of Lilian Baylis of the Old Vic, a name which reverberates like a bell. But for how long? The names of Adolphe Appia and Gordon Craig shine as silver—though the commercial theatre can never pay the debt it owes them. Dullin and Copeau, great names, were working till their deaths, though do you know which one of them died in a public ward, with scarcely enough money to pay his funeral? What of William Poel who, as they say, 'discovered' Edith Evans (which is to say little more than can be said for the man who sees the first magical, surprising swallow in spring) but who left a generation or more of actors and producers understanding Shakespeare as they had never understood it before? Poel, who lived to be old, successfully directed the Old Vic when only 29 for two years from 1881-1883, and yet was never asked to do so again? What of the *Compagnie des Quinze?* What of the Abbey Theatre? Granville-Barker, a bold spirit if ever there was one, retired into the resounding shell of his prefaces and lectures. These names echo still. But some of you have never heard of Leslie Faber, who, it is true, was a popular, high-paid 'star'-actor, but so complete an artist that he could appear in two leading parts in the same play without the audience knowing of it. And though he died more recently, how many of you remember Morland Graham, of whom Charles Lamb could have written an essay all for himself?

These were 'Protean' actors, if you like, yet by no means what Walkley would have called 'mere mimes'. The protagonists of Proteus pay a high price. Signing away that intensification of their own personalities, we remember them not as one person but as many. It is harder to remember many than one. Nevertheless, the very unselfishness of their approach gives to their work a kind of purity which blesses it.

I will not ask you to remember all these names—though many of them will be known to you—but suggest instead that you choose your own touchstones, that you should ask yourself the same sort of question that Longinus, the Athenian master of rhetoric at the Syrian Court of Palmyra over sixteen hundred years ago, asked his pupils. Longinus recommended them to find a touchstone for their compositions, bidding them ask, 'How would my work be received by Homer or Demosthenes?'

Who is your Homer? Who your Demosthenes?

I shall not try to answer the first two questions that I put to you just now; about the full function of the actor and 'How far is that function fulfilled in our modern theatre?' I shall leave you to infer what answers I have to these.

But 'How far does the modern theatre frustrate him?' can be answered quite simply: to the extent that it forces him to be a casual labourer. To be sure, writers, composers, painters, poets are also casual labourers, but at least their means of creation are always at hand. No, the interpretative artist knows the meaning of frustration, if not more deeply, certainly more often than they.

'How far does the actor himself frustrate the theatre's function?' Stanislavski said that the fact that the theatre so often loses both its power and its dignity was chiefly due to the actors themselves. He ascribed to the actors the blame for the introduction of the worst abominations in the theatre, such as gossip, slander, envy, intrigue and selfish ambition. He warned his actors against such lack of self-control and such disrespect towards what should be their temple, the theatre, that they should ever be so uncivilised as—for instance—

to wash their dirty linen in public. This warning was especially necessary, since the only kind of theatre for which he wished was the theatre in which everything depends on the collective work of the ensemble. (11)

As Michael Chehov rightly said, there are three ways of playing a scene: to concentrate on explaining and demonstrating everything to the audience, or to put on a performance for oneself, or to play for and with the other actors in the scene. There will be more to say about the disastrous second of these alternatives (which is to play a scene for oneself) in the third lecture when we come to the subject of feeling and emotion. As for the first method—to play to the audience—well, we have to admit that it is still quite common. For the third, to play for and to one's partners, which rightly, Michael Chehov says, is the best method, how beautifully often can one now see this! It is a cliché of criticism to remark how exquisitely a certain actor or actress 'listens'. But it is a cliché founded on a very true and valuable fact, and one can think of many notable examples of its practice.

No, though there may be some bad examples to the contrary, the most notable of our English actors and actresses are primarily men and women of the theatre and, contrary to some critical belief, I cannot think that this change has in any way diminished the value of their acting.

I began this discursion on ethics in the theatre with the name of Stanislavski and I will end with a quotation from the same source, for he adjures every actor to 'love the art in himself, and not himself in art.'

A little high-faluting, some may think, or an easy and effective paradox. For such as think so, hear the concluding words of the same quotation: 'Love the art in yourself, and not yourself in art,' says Stanislavski, 'for this leads to success in our work.'

Where does the actor stand in relation to the author, the producer, the public? What of dramatic tradition? The actor's relations with the author I will leave till much later, his attitude towards the public I have already touched on and will do so again to-morrow. Which leaves us with the producer and dramatic tradition, which are commonly allied.

I said just now that the star actor had to some extent abdicated from his illogical nineteenth-century throne and that some kind of peaceful revolution had, as it were, taken place. Oddly enough— though not surprisingly when you come to think of it—during the same term of revolution, the producer, whose function was previously carried out by the star actor or the stage manager, has achieved a hitherto unheard-of prominence and become in many cases the autocratic head of state. I am well aware even as I speak these words that they may sound not a little reactionary. For the years when he was a dramatic critic, Bernard Shaw constantly pleaded for the abdication of the star actor and the accession of a controlling mind in production which would ensure against the exploitation of the author.(12)

Shaw did as much as any man to bring about a revolution in the theatre itself and in the public taste which he educated—not so much by his dramatic criticisms but by his plays themselves—to prefer a play of ideas or a play for ensemble-acting to the fashionable 19th century star-vehicle. And it is worth noting that with a few exceptions towards the end of the nineteenth century, very few of these vehicles are nowadays ever trotted out from the stable. Shaw, Poel and Granville-Barker were among the most notable names who brought about the shift in literary-theatrical taste which resulted in the public preferring to see a play as a whole. (Paradoxically it is also worth noting that the plays of these authors now most generally esteemed are the ones which can be called 'star-vehicles'.)

The wheel has turned a little and during the last 50 years we have seen a very strange assortment of producers' experiments. Now a producer has similar tendencies to that of any other creative or interpretative artist. He tends to do more and more the thing that comes easiest to him and that he can do best; or, on a lower level, to do again what he has previously found to be successful. The Duke of Saxe-Meiningen was the first producer to establish his control of crowds on the stage, and since then the capacity to handle large numbers of actors in a lively and exciting manner has become the hallmark of a certain kind of producer. Given enough people and sufficient time, the effective handling of crowds is not in itself a very remarkable achievement. The less so if the producer has no particular care for the author's words but is content to dazzle the eye. Nearly all such producers, having to choose between ear and eye, will plump for the eye. Nearly all such producers tend to become highly autocratic. Such a one was Reinhardt, with his enormous *Regiebücher*, in which almost every detail of the performance, of movement, of pause, etc., was laid down, sometimes in advance and inexorably.(13)

Now the actor is a very 'suggestible' person, so much so that even if one or two chance acquaintances make the same criticism of his performance he will be tempted to change it. Such a man is only too ready to believe a very self-confident producer and everything he tells him, the more so today when the actor and actress are educated in the belief that the producer's word is law.

And if the producer's word is not law, whose word is to be? The actor's? The day of the actor-manager, it seems, is past. What, in fact, happens in practice nowadays, at any rate in some of the better productions, is that not only do the leading actors and producer confer for as long a time as is possible in the conditions of our theatre, but when the other parts are cast, the producer will —unless he is type-casting, in which case there is little for him to say—suggest as clearly as possible to the actors the kind of way he wants them to play their parts. Of course it does not all work as smoothly as that sounds. For one thing, the producer's idea may not prove to be as clear and workable as he had thought it was on paper. It is also very tempting sometimes for an actor, especially if he may have been out of work for some time, to try to give a twist or emphasis to his part which will make it stand out more prominently than the author intended.

It was observed by the great French actor Coquelin that the English actors had one of the defects of our national virtues which is, he said, a passion for originality. This would have seemed even more striking to Coquelin than it does to us now, for in Coquelin's day some of the teachers at the Comédie Française were still insisting that there was such a thing as:

La seule inflexion juste.

We have never known or even contemplated such a state of affairs here, and while making due allowances for the difference between French classical alexandrines, which are much more rigid than our dramatic blank verse, it can only be said to be good that it is so. But then we are a nation that is singular in its complete break with a theatrical tradition historically as well as temperamentally. I have sometimes thought that Cromwell's purgatory must have been to be a stage-doorkeeper.

Some 30 years ago much was known by old actors about what was called 'traditional business' in Shakespeare or in the eighteenth-century classical comedies. But about that time, when the modern producer had really begun to get into his stride, anything that savoured of tradition became anathema. On the whole this was good, for much if not most of this was an accretion of business taken over from older actors, most of which had long lost its point.

Now it is my impression that today the young actor would rather be seen dead than using somebody else's idea. Yet Irving, about to play Robert Macaire, a part made famous by Frédéric Lemaitre, could write to Percy Fitzgerald:

> You said . . . you might have a few bits of business of the immortal Frédéric. I never saw that great master, but everything he did would be well worth consideration(14).

and you will find that Sir Laurence Olivier, in an introduction to a new edition of a Shakespeare tragedy, can talk of 'plodding diligently through the more comprehensive histories of the various performances.'(15) Such actors would be eager rather than afraid to know what others had done before them in the same field, and by no means ashamed to borrow, or rather inherit; being conscious of their own originality, which gives the creative actor a deed of inheritance.

In the same way an actor need not be afraid of theory, once he is conscious of his latent powers.

Theory and method, as I hope to be able to indicate, are of immense value to the actor who can translate them into practice. They are also, there can be no doubt, toxic to the actor who cannot.

They should be labelled 'as prescribed by the physician.' But at
their worst they are never as poisonous as convention. The con-
ventional actor suffers a growing paralysis for which there is, after
a time, no known cure.

It is a good sign of our theatre today that so many a young
actor and actress is not content to be what Jouvet meant by *un
acteur*, but chooses rather the harder but infinitely more rewarding
task of the *comédien*.

It is a good sign also, I think, that we are at last emerging from
the era of the naturalistic play, and of the school of acting which
has been described, not unfairly, as the school of behaving.[16] This
school has been taken over by the cinema, where some of the most
convincing performances are given by people who are not actors
at all. When the word 'actuality' first came into use, it gave the
logical as well as practical quietus to the quietist school.

I know of the dangers of making parallels with other arts, but
just as the basic quality of a picture is *how it is painted*—not its
subject, style nor school, not the genius or personality of the painter
nor his mood at the time—though all these may contribute to the
final value of the picture; and just as Stendhal insisted: 'Le roman
doit raconter', and again: 'La première qualité d'un roman doit
être: raconter . . .'; and in much the same way as we speak of 'pure
music,' so there is what we could call, if the term were not debased,
'Pure Theatre'. In its debased sense we mean, of course, melodrama,
theatricality—hokum, call it what you will. But there is a reason
why a dramatist must write a play rather than a novel, just as there
is a cogent reason why a poet should choose to write poetry rather
than prose. It is in this sense that I ask you to understand what I
mean by, and what I can only call, 'Pure Theatre'. It is the 'Pure
Theatre' which Shakespeare understood; the theatre which, I
would guess, the Greeks understood; which Molière understood.
The basic value of theatrical writing is *theatre*.

The basis of acting—and I wish to make myself as clear as I can
on this point—the basis of acting is nothing more nor less than
acting. I do not mean what has been called 'the old one, two, three,'
but I mean something remarkably like it.

'The old one, two, three' is crude, but it is up to a point
effective. I know at least one old actress who cannot enter an

ordinary room without 'making an entrance', and if she has nothing to say she will exhale the syllable 'ah,' by which she 'lifts the scene' and 'sets the mood' (her mood, of course). The last thirty years or so have changed all that. We have seen the rise of a more naturalistic school of acting in the presence of which older play-goers have been known to exclaim that they could neither see a thing nor hear a word.

On the two following occasions I will try to examine some of the theories of the actor's craft; his preliminary studies; his tech-nique; his processes of thought; his relation with his subconscious; but the essence of acting, I repeat, is the power to act. Thought or emotion may or may not be present—but the basic will of the actor must be, quite simply, to act: not to think, not to feel, not to exhibitionise, not to make some personal statement—though he may do one or all of these—*but to act*. This is a point which at the present time and in the conditions of this address cannot be made too forcefully. It is as compelling as the word to 'open fire'. The curtain is up. Go on and act. How this is done, what precedes it, what accompanies it, what lends it any such dignity as it may claim, but above all what gives it force and meaning, will be my subject from now.

II

Instinct and Method—I

I BELIEVE that most of the great practitioners of the theatre have, whether they have made it known or otherwise, given considerable thought both to what they were doing and to the consequent effect. It is a truism that actors are born and not made; another truism that acting cannot be taught. The basis of all acting is undoubtedly instinctive, but that does not mean that a great deal of this is not susceptible to some kind of analysis, or that method may not make more than it mars.

The history of drama, like the history of the world, is in part a history of delayed action.

In the history of the theatre, time frequently lags to a seeming standstill. Even now it is commonly assumed that acting is done merely by the light of nature, a nightly phenomenon—and why should such a delusion not exist, since one of the aims of acting is to appear to be lit only in that light? It is still supposed in some quarters that, let us say, the famous, I would almost say the notorious, 'Method' of Stanislavski was something which pertained entirely to Russia and the plays of Chehov at the turn of the century and that any relics of it now are mere out-moded æstheticism. But this is not so. Stanislavski's theories, which were based on experience; the theories of William Poel, to which I shall make special reference in the fourth lecture; the theories of Granville-Barker and the pictorial theories of Gordon Craig, have all had their widest effect long after the germ of their ideas was first sown.

There is Stanislavski, whose ideas were taken and transplanted all over Europe and to America, where they found some of their best expression in the work of the Group Theatre in the 1920s and '30s, which has influenced most of the 'poetic realism' of the modern American theatre, and which survives in the work of Elia Kazan and his Actors' Studio in New York. It is impossible to trace all that has been directly or indirectly influenced by the great

Russian director and his work with the Moscow Art Theatre. It has crossed and re-crossed boundaries, it has echoed from shore to shore. In France, for instance, it seized the imagination of the young Jacques Copeau. Copeau learnt from it and adapted it to his needs, and he in his turn taught and worked with Michel St. Denis; and through St. Denis—a great director, a great artist, a great man —who with his founding of the London Theatre Studio before the war and of the Old Vic School and the Young Vic after the war, created our only schools of acting which were fundamentally true, imaginative and thorough—through St. Denis—and therefore through Copeau, through Dullin, through Stanislavski, we have, in many actors and actresses, designers, producers and authors, here amongst us, now, the seed, the flower and fruit of some of the best in our theatre of today and tomorrow.

We should remember this. Theatrical history will say that Michel St. Denis left England in 1952 to return to France, and I have no doubt that theatrical history will add that in Strasbourg, where he is about to launch a new French company in a new theatre, St. Denis wrote another fine chapter in the history of the theatre. But, alas for us, not in our theatre. His previous chapter —'Michel St. Denis en Angleterre'—may sound a little inconclusive, at least in print, though it certainly had its glories. There will be those who will not understand that it was not St. Denis' wish to leave this country. Perhaps they will not even care. At least, as the years go on, they will care less. You will perceive that the tone of this address has become more personal. It is with excuse and reason. If I go on to add that it was due to a lack of foresight on the part of the Governors and the Director of the Old Vic at that time—a lack of foresight which amounted to folly, for it is folly, in art, to speed the departure of those who are truly great—it is because I can think of no more telling example of how our theatre, that fascinating dangerous jungle, will, if it can, resist, and finally banish the artist whom it considers austere, or too original, or too uncompromising. It is significant, not only in our theatre, but in others, that Poel, Granville-Barker, Appia and Craig all more or less retired from the working theatre as they found it in their day. In each of these cases we might feel that their theories were too far in advance of their practice, that they were revolutionaries without the power to effect revolution. But in fact, perhaps indirectly, but certainly, they did effect their several revolutions.

Their revolutions were, as the best revolutions are, not only bloodless, but gradual.

Looking back in time, on, as we may now call it, the horizontal level, we tend to think that most of the great artists had success in their lifetimes. It is not so. Stendhal, for example, who had many gifts, and who in his lifetime can scarcely be considered a failure in the worldly sense, prophesied that his writings would be understood and properly appreciated years after his death. To be on the safe side he named several dates. They were all correct. In 1912 William Poel, who was regarded by many as a cranky amateur, induced a young woman from a milliner's shop in Bond Street to play in a few performances of *Troilus and Cressida*, presented in the Poel version of the Elizabethan style. George Moore and one or two others wrote enthusiastically of the production and of the young woman's performance. The young milliner decided not to go back to her millinery. She learnt what she could from Poel and his theories of dramatic speech. She realises and acknowledges still what she owes to the man whom some called a 'cranky amateur.' Few among the thousands who saw the actress for whom James Bridie wrote *Daphne Laureola* realise that the magic of that performance was largely the magic of verbal control, the understanding and manipulation of words. We talk of her personality, her magnetism, her wonderful assumption of beauty, all of which she has in abundance. They are so compelling that the audience does not analyse the result. That is just as it should be. Analysis is not part of the function of the audience, nor does it always add to its pleasure.

It was remarked recently by a dramatic critic that it is not so easy

> to discuss the theatre academically. There the theoretical is constantly being brought up with a bump against stubborn realities. The audience is one of these—predominantly out for a distracting evening and comfortably unadvanced—and you cannot, except by a sublime act of faith, disregard the audience entirely.(17)

Mr. Worsley was writing as a theatre critic about theatre criticism. I use his words as preface in the hope that they may make my own

BEROWNE

in *Love's Labour's Lost*
Old Vic Theatre
Company,
New Theatre, 1950

John Vickers

YOUNG MARLOWE

in *She Stoops to Conquer*
with Diana Churchill
Old Vic Theatre
Company,
New Theatre, 1950

John Vickers

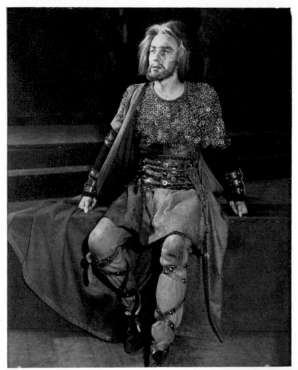

MACBETH

Aldwych Theatre, London, and National Theatre, New York, 1948

Hugelmeyer, New York

ORIN

in the film *Mourning Becomes Electra*. R.K.O., Hollywood, 1947

sound more objective. But I especially like the sentence, 'You cannot, except by a sublime act of faith, disregard the audience entirely.'

Now it has been suggested by an actor that the actor's primary feeling towards his audience should be one of 'benevolence and bounty mixed with gratitude'.(18) We have been called, and we call ourselves, the servants of the public:

> The drama's laws the drama's patrons give
> For we who live to please must please to live.

That is, perhaps, how we would like the public to think of us, most of the time. After all, it implies that we can always say that if we have failed to please we have still, as good professional actors, done our best. But is that the whole truth? Could it be that sometimes we only pretend to please to live? The actor must at all times be more generous than his audience. But I do not think 'gratitude' is what is felt. Not at least during performance.

A question that is put with not insignificant monotony to players who act for both stage and screen—it follows the monotonous and less significant question of, 'Which do you prefer?'—is usually, 'Don't you miss the audience?' My own answer is usually, 'No: why should I? I do not miss the audience at rehearsals when the character is being created, and some of the most exciting moments of creative acting take place at rehearsals.' I confess that is an evasive answer, for the simple, logical retort to it would be, 'Surely you do not wish to go on rehearsing for ever?' My reply to this is an emphatic, 'Certainly not.' But it is a fallacy to believe, as I have previously mentioned in this talk, that the audience is *ipso facto* of assistance to the actor. It can betray him into seeking easy ways to please, repeating blandishments which he knows have been previously successful. It can force him to seek to dominate their mood, as he is frequently obliged to do, with force or tricks which are alien to the part he is playing. It can, in short, make him a flatterer or a fighting madman. 'To please the ears of the ground-lings' has become 'To play to the gallery.'

I do not suggest that an actor should be a Coriolanus who, through his pride in his own integrity, should never speak the soft word that will win the heart. But I do say that though the audience may bring a stronger pressure on him than either his author, his producer or his own artistic conscience, it should never force him to be faithless to these three. Perhaps what I am really trying to say is that he must find his own artistic conscience. A faith in what he thinks and hopes he can do. And this applies not only to actors who have high ambitions—for the actor, like other artists, must sooner or later have some sense of his own limitations—it applies to all actors. I think it was Hazlitt who remarked that 'whatever a man can do well, is worth doing.' The artistic conscience—or if you prefer it—a man's integrity, demands that what he does he should also do well. Yesterday, when I quoted the lines about 'love the art in yourself, and not yourself in art', I tried to suggest that it was essential to actors, as to other artists, to acquire the strength of humility. I do not think it is contradictory to requote also the words of Sarah Bernhardt to her students: 'You must always think of what pleases *you*. It is up to you to be demanding, severe, a person of taste'. What bridges that apparent contradiction is integrity.

Just as there is a dualism in the nature of every actor, there is also a dualism in any audience. It is a fallacy to suppose that even an average audience, if there is such a thing, comes to a play with an open mind. It comes bristling with a variety of prejudices. It is one of the functions of the drama to allay these prejudices and to leave the audience with a more open mind and heart. But before it allays it must agitate. Just as Baudelaire addressed his readers: 'Hypocrite lecteur! Mon Semblable! Mon Frère!' so the actor and the drama must do also: he must *challenge* and *at the same time embrace* his audience, he must say, in effect:

Hypocrite spectateur! Mon Semblable! Mon Frère!

But how does the actor challenge, or at any rate embrace, an audience whom he can scarcely see?

It has been noticed for some time now that the 'picture stage' not only does not answer the requirements of all kinds of plays but that it creates a barrier between the lighted player and his darkened audience. Voices have been shouting, 'Away with it'. Recent experiments, especially with the platform or arena type of stage, have shown that a great variety of plays can be satisfactorily performed in the middle of an audience. Though in my opinion the 'arena' stage suits best plays of movement and action and a broad style, I have seen staged, in an arena type theatre in California, a performance of a naturalistic play, *Ethan Frome*, with only three characters, and it certainly came over well enough. It did not, it is true, have very far to come. The auditorium in this case was tiny, and here the problem seemed to be reversed: instead of the actor having to project across a barrier it seemed as if the audience, who felt as if they were almost in the same room with the actors, were trying not to intrude on a personal domestic tragedy. The actors muted themselves to the proportions of the cinema. This was, however, a special case and not truly representative of the experiments which have been made on these lines. But to my mind, speaking as an actor, these experiments remain illogical unless we flood not only the stage but the auditorium with light.

In 1939 I was playing in Michel St. Denis' production of *Twelfth Night* at the Phoenix Theatre. Though there were many beauties in the production it was not a success, and to quote Jouvet again, 'Le seul problème du théâtre, c'est le succès.' The play was very beautifully lighted by George Devine who is, amongst other things, a master of lighting. And when I say it was beautifully lit I do not mean that it was 'artily' lit, for it is notorious that in 'arty' lighting, or indeed in any lighting in which the producer tries to paint the scenery rather than light actors, the actors will tend to find shadows for themselves, as it were. I do not mean by that that they will not instinctively try to find the best light but that in lighting which is composed of high-lights and half-lights and shadows the actor, oddly enough, tunes the key of his performance more to the shadows than to the high-lights. This was made very clear on this occasion by an odd coincidence. This production of *Twelfth Night* was one of the first plays which the B.B.C. televised in its entirety from a London theatre, and for the occasion a special audience was invited—though I think people were allowed to buy tickets—because the setting up of the different television cameras and the installation of very bright, hard television lights could not be expected to give the same effect as we had planned in the production of the play.

The first thing that happened was that all the actors spoke louder, acted in a broader style and projected their performances with a great deal more vigour. There was twice as much laughter, for instance, at the comedy scenes, and not, I think, because some of the audience was specially invited (for outside the B.B.C. invited audiences are usually considered 'dead-heads'), but because the comedy passages were twice as funny.

Though I have witnessed a number of them, I do not go with alacrity to open-air performances. This, I suppose, is partly because since I was a child I have been conditioned to think of a theatre, almost any theatre, as the most magical place in any town. Also, I have never been able to understand why the circling of pigeons over Alexander Moissi's head as he played Everyman in front of the cathedral in Salzburg, or the twittering of London sparrows and starlings during the performance of *A Midsummer Night's Dream* in Regent's Park, or a glorious sunset over the courtyard at Kronborg during the yearly performances of *Hamlet*, should in any way add to the theatrical value of these occasions. But one has to face the fact that to many people these adventitious circumstances seem not only to add to but to increase the value of the performance. However, when it happened that I was asked with the Old Vic to play *Hamlet* in the vast courtyard of Kronborg Castle—admittedly far too vast and acoustically very poor—I felt again as I had during the television relay of *Twelfth Night*. We had to speak up and act up to the height of our powers and I found myself exceeding what I had hitherto supposed were my powers in both these directions. Incidentally, after playing ten performances of *Hamlet* in the open-air at Elsinore, we then opened with it in a fairly large theatre in Amsterdam, and I discovered that for the first time I felt I had more voice, variety of tone and inflection even than I needed for the part. But of course in the open air, and even if Kronborg courtyard were half the size it is, much of this variety of inflection and any subtleties of expression had to be abandoned. I have noticed the same thing in all open-air performances that I have seen.

It may be there can be little doubt that the picture-stage has overstayed its welcome—though under the present fire-laws and other restrictions we are likely to see quite a lot of it for the rest of our lifetimes—it has served to do what it set out to do, which is to concentrate the spectator's attention on the actors and to permit the actor (and through him the author) a variety and subtlety and intensification which are very difficult to achieve without it.

Now it is only since the advent of the picture-stage that we have any records of individual style or method in acting. We do not assume, of course, that none existed, but the art of playing was, until less than three centuries ago, founded on the art of oratory which, coupled with the actor's temperament, the ability to 'fly to it like French falconers', mainly carried the day. Rehearsals must have been scanty, 'production' was largely a matter of convention, and there can have been little time for subtleties.

This idea that, granted a touch of genius or talent or even luck, everything 'will be all right on the night,' is something which has only disappeared from our stage in the last century. Even now it has not completely gone, but it has considerably diminished since the days when 'star' actors were phenomena who descended, usually with very few rehearsals and sometimes with only one or two, on a 'stock' company who had been rehearsed in their roles by the stage manager, and who obediently grouped themselves round the star while he held the centre stage. You have only to look at the architecture of many English theatres still in use to realise that nothing of any significance could ever have been played outside what we call 'left or right centre.'

In the preparation of a part, both at rehearsal and especially at the nightly performance, the question of mood is of first importance. Unless the actor is on that particular evening wishing above everything else in the world to act, that performance may be reasonably good but it is unlikely to be his best. To act well and to act well repeatedly has to become an obsession. I am not qualified to judge what it is that makes certain men and women liable to this obsession, through which they obtain pre-eminence as actors. Obviously some psychological reason exists, and equally obviously some day a book will be written about it by a psychologist explaining the whole matter. It will probably 'debunk' all acting, and most actors and actresses, including myself, will resolutely refuse to read it.

Generally speaking, the mood necessary to play comedy is easier to achieve than the mood for drama or tragedy, perhaps because comedy brings a release and a relief from the cares of daily life. It is therefore only too easy for one gifted with a player's temperament to enter a world of make-believe in which he will experience a well-being and sense of happiness and fun which he may not have felt since he woke up that morning.

Now it is a general opinion that it is harder to play comedy than tragedy, and Garrick is quoted as saying that to succeed in tragedy one must first succeed in comedy. These opinions need a little sifting, I think. Perhaps for the inexperienced actor it is harder to achieve that confidence and ease, especially in timing, which are essential to playing comedy, and if that is so it explains Garrick's remark. But in my own experience I know that I find that to wake up in the morning knowing I am to play Aguecheek, or Young Marlowe, or Berowne—or Hotspur even—gives me a lightness of spirit which allows me even to become absorbed in other things, whereas if it is a night for Hamlet, Macbeth or Richard II, more than a small part of myself is, as it were, in attendance all day.

In the playing of tragedy or of heavy dramatic parts, the approach cannot exactly be laid down. It remains largely a matter of instinct though the germ of the Stanislavski method is to help the actor discover the creative mood, to clear the decks for action. As I say, an actor or an actress playing a great or heavy part at night is to some extent oppressed with the sense of that duty all day. They may be gay, witty, grave or trivial during certain moments of that day, but always, unconsciously, they know that at night they have an experience to live through which, if they do not prepare themselves to meet it, will leave them unsatisfied and defeated. And the fluctuations of this mood are extraordinary. It might seem, to take a crude example, that the best preparation for playing Hamlet would be to spend an intensely unhappy day, preferably worrying about one's father or mother. Not at all. The actor can spend an extremely gay and amusing day and by sheer contrast, the moment when he has to put on the sober suit of solemn black can intensify

Hamlet's grief. What he cannot do is to spend a day forgetful that at night he plays Hamlet.

It is said by one of her biographers that Eleonora Duse used to spend the days on which she was going to play Ibsen's *The Lady from the Sea* gazing out from her hotel bedroom at the Mediterranean. That is very appealing nonsense, and to do justice to Duse, I am sure that this is an elaboration by her biographer. Perhaps once, playing in Genoa, she sat looking out at the Mediterranean. And perhaps out of politeness she allowed this same biographer to think that she was putting herself in the mood for the play. But what did Duse do when she played *The Lady from the Sea* in Milan?

Now Duse was obviously a creature who by temperament could sustain intensity for long hours, even days at a stretch. Probably her desire to gaze at the sea was one way of relaxing. (I live overlooking a river and I know how it draws one to the windows to gaze at it.) But the whole purpose of off-stage relaxation for the actor is 'reculer pour mieux sauter'.

Jouvet had said that 'le trac' or 'stage-fright' is something that the good actor will know how to turn to his advantage. That is true. But commonly we associate 'stage-fright' or 'nerves' only with first nights. A degree of 'nerves' or 'insecurity' is valuable every night, especially in dramatic parts. It is a state of body and mind, a mood that is very difficult to describe. One must not be tense, for tension is inhibiting, but one's state of relaxation or calm must be charged with purpose. One only knows, by experience, that on certain nights one achieves it, without effort, that on others one has to wait patiently for it to come, that sometimes it comes and goes, and that sometimes it does not come at all. Now there can be no doubt that when it comes—'Cette grace'—as Jouvet called it— the actor can surpass himself. Its chief characteristic is the ease with which everything can be done. Sir Malcolm Sargent once told me that the question a conductor is most frequently asked is, 'Doesn't it give you a wonderful feeling of power to conduct a big orchestra?' His reply is that on the contrary, when the orchestra is playing well it gives only a sense of ease, when not, a feeling of frustration. When it does not come—'cette grace'—one can only say, as Mounet-Sully said after a performance which did not please him: 'Ce soir, le dieu n'est pas venu'.

Now the chief interest of all this is that even to a keen observer of the play, even if he has seen it several times, there is no very marked difference between the performance when the actor knows he is having to make an effort and the evening when the 'god' comes. I say no very marked difference in the sense that it would be hard for any but a constant and professional observer to lay a finger on where the difference lay.

But there is, all the same, a difference. If there were none, then Coquelin, who claimed not only that the actor need not feel but that he should not feel, would be right. It would remain entirely a question of technique. But the evenings of grace, when 'the god' is there, those are the evenings when acting is truly an art. In case any of you are wondering which of the many gods this god might be I will say that I think he might be Apollo.

All this is another way of saying that the great moments or evenings in the theatre, those which leave the strongest impression on the spectator, often arise from the unconscious of the player and are not susceptible to analysis either by him or by the beholder. As it has been put, in yet another way, these are the times when his playing achieves 'rhythm', when we can say that the performance has 'flight', or 'leaves the ground'.

But these occasions mostly happen when the preliminary work has been deeply felt and composed with at least some conscious care. We actors frequently like to give the impression that the whole composition is, as it were, inspired from within and that there is nothing of the deliberate about it. This may be partly our vanity, or it may be the very natural and proper desire to conceal our methods or tricks in the belief that if the spectator knew how they worked they would cease to impress or deceive him. Nevertheless the biographies, journals and letters that actors have left us bear witness to an infinite degree of care, especially over small details. I imagine that the mind processes of the actor at this stage are similar to the work of a detective. He does not set about, like a police inspector, simply to gather every bit of evidence for its own sake as a matter of routine, but like Sherlock Holmes, or the detective Maigret created by the novelist Simenon, he shifts the available evidence around in his mind rather as one might shift the pieces of a jig-saw puzzle until by some instinct he finds himself in possession of a psychological clue or characteristic which will suddenly illuminate the whole character for him, and help him find the truth.

The truth for him, that is. It does not, of course, follow that he will always be right; indeed it is only the detectives of fiction who are always right. And what do we mean by 'right' in this case? We mean right in the sense that it fits both the circumstances offered by the author—the scene of the crime—and what we might call the personality and motives of the criminal—that is, the character. Like a detective, also, the actor has often to turn over and discard a hundred or more clues for one that may be of use to him, and he can never be certain at what point this valuable clue will appear. There is also no knowing the nature of the clue. Sometimes it is to do with appearances of face, figure or even costume; sometimes it is a tone of voice or a trick of speech; sometimes even, it can be a mere 'prop'. These are usually best found by instinct. That is why, especially in the preparation of the great parts, a considerable amount of time should be allowed before rehearsals during which a part of the actor's mind lies fallow, while a small questing part of it keeps first the shape of the play and then the general idea of the character either in his conscious thoughts or just below consciousness. It has been said that the period of gestation for a great part is the same as for that of a child: nine months.

There is a delightful story of Irving at the time when he was about to undertake *King Lear*. He and Graham Robertson, who tells the story,(19) were taking a holiday by the sea in Cornwall:

> Once, during a walk when we were discussing some totally different subject—probably dogs—he stopped and, gazing fixedly at me, demanded: 'Where am I going to get that feather from?'
> 'Feather?'
> 'Yes. *You* know—when I say, "This feather stirs. She lives." What am I doing with a feather in my hand? Where did it come from? Did you ever see *Lear* acted?'
> 'No,' I said.
> 'That's a pity: you might have remembered. I saw in a book

that Macready used to pluck the feather out of Edgar's helmet, but I can't do that.'

'Why not?' I enquired.

'Why not? Why, if I started plucking feathers out of William Terriss the whole house would roar. What *can* I do?'

We sat down and became gradually aware of feathers, quantities of feathers, lying about on the grass.

'Here are feathers,' said Irving slowly. 'Any amount of 'em—and the scene is by the sea—just like this. I'll have a feather tacked to the stage cloth just where I kneel beside Cordelia; then I can pick it up and—there I am.'

He gathered up a few feathers thoughtfully.

Next day I found him near the same spot, his handkerchief full of feathers.

'I'm going to keep them and use them in *Lear*,' he said, displaying his take. 'I shall like to feel that they were picked up by the sea—real seabirds' feathers.'

I inspected the collection. 'Ye-es,' I said regretfully. 'But you know, those are all *hens*' feathers. They've blown out of that yard—somebody has been plucking a fowl.'

'Ah,' said Irving with one of his curious staccato grunts, and emptied his handkerchief. The feathers had lost their powers of inspiration—why could I not have held my tongue?

Irving's productions were nothing if not representational, and though the idea of feathers—even seagulls' feathers—tacked about the Lyceum stage to give point to one line may offend our modern views of production, the story helps to illustrate the kind of small chance which may clear or cloud an actor's imagination.

It is interesting to note here that this kind of attention to detail is a characteristic of our English temperament, and we can remember that the great French actor Coquelin remarked that by national temperament English actors tended to be too original:

. . . when Talma appeared he made tragedy natural, and to that he owed his success and his influence.

Was his naturalness that of Garrick? I cannot tell. The genius of the two races is too different; the love of originality is too strong with our neighbours for them always to remain within the true measure of things; . . .(20)

I was recently chided for this when in a cycle of four Histories at Stratford-on-Avon in 1951 I played Harry Hotspur and assumed an approximation of the Northumbrian country accent, partly in order to justify Lady Percy's lines about Hotspur, after his death, which mention that he was 'thick of speech'. To me, the dialect, which I acquired with the help of various inhabitants of Northumberland and a recording-machine, was of enormous aid, since it took me right outside myself and also made the strongest possible contrast to the tones of Richard II which I was playing in each preceding performance. I was aware, of course, that 'thick of speech' does not necessarily mean the thick 'rs' of Northumbrian speech—though since none of the authorities agree on what 'thick of speech' does mean I felt justified in offering this alternative.

And to the somewhat niggling criticism that it was odd that Harry Percy's father, Northumberland, and the other nobles such as Westmoreland, did not also talk in country speech, I had what seemed to me the perfectly good answer that it was never said of them that they were 'thick of speech', also that Harry Hotspur's first appearance, which is in *Richard II*, shows that he does not even know what Bolingbroke looks like, for he fails to recognise him, which would argue that he has not been around the Court until manhood and that even in *Henry IV: Part I* we find in Hotspur's first scene at Court that he does not know that King Richard had named his cousin Mortimer as his successor.

The next time we see him he is back at Warkworth—the ruins of which still stand by the Northumberland coast—calling for his horse, and Prince Hal's description of him, where he mimics him, saying, 'give my roan horse a drench', implies a man who spends most of his time in the country. We later know, in the scene with Glendower, that he has no ear for verse and that he prides himself on it.

But all this secondary argument on my part would be of no avail whatever if the dialect speech did not 'come off'. I think I can say that on the whole it did, and that after the first shock of surprise the average audience was prepared to believe that such a character would have talked in that way. But if it did not come off, then no amount of reasoning on my part would be to the slightest point, for reasoning does not enter into a theatrical experience, however

much it may be of use occasionally in its preparation. This is
what the French call *optique du théâtre* and it is a very sound phrase
to bear in mind. In point of fact I was not lacking in *optique du
théâtre* in the wider sense, for, as you will remember, *Henry IV: Part I*
was played as part of the tetralogy ranging from *Richard II* to *Henry
V*, and it was part of the producers' plan—and I was one of the
producers—to restore Prince Hal to his proper status as the hero of
the last three plays. To this end we not only deliberately and, I
think, rightly, gave due emphasis to all the more sordid side of
Falstaff, which mitigates Prince Hal's rejection of him in *Part II*,
but I deliberately set out not to make Hotspur the romantic hero
of *Part I* as he is usually played by the star actor.

But what, you may well ask, has this kind of thing—instinct,
mood, thought-processes, the search for a clue—to do with method?

These are all personal to different actors, and in acting the
achievement does not survive the creator. In other arts we form
and maintain certain standards by making 'a reservoir of classic
precept in the work of great masters'.(21)   It can still be said today,
in the sense that Lessing said in the eighteenth century, that we have
actors, but no art of acting.

The student or teacher who attempts to go back to the beginnings
of the history of method in acting needs a stout heart and a clear
head. One of the oldest signposts points us back to the study of
oratory and rhetoric. We should be wary of this signpost. Not
only because it leads us back so far in time and place, to Syracuse,
five hundred years before Christ, where we are told the Greek,
Corax, first recognised and taught oratory as an art. Not only
because on the return journey we would have to make a long stop
with Aristotle, whose *Rhetoric* became the textbook for centuries,
and who, in sum, sponsored Rhetoric as the servant of virtue—for
the consideration of this alliance of Rhetoric and virtue might be
of some interest to us today. It might be interesting, too, to chat
with Dionysius of Halicarnassus (we are already some 450 years
on our return journey), for Dionysius was one of the earliest to
exemplify that function of criticism which consists of discerning
enjoyment rather than judgment by pre-ordained rules—yes, I

think if we had the time we might want to ask Dionysius what he meant by enjoyment, for that sounds perhaps a little nearer what we are after. Longinus' *On the Sublime* was, I remember, one of the parts of Professor Saintsbury's *Loci Critici*, which was recommended reading in the English tripos when I was an undergraduate, and it might be pleasant to remember what Longinus said . . . but I will not pretend off-hand that I do. Leaving him and with a passing wave of the hand to three orators whom, if we know the theatre, we like to think of as old friends of ours—Brutus, Caesar and Marcus Antonius—we might call at the house of one who, though he lived in the first century A.D., had great influence on mediaeval and renaissance students, a man with a most euphonious name, Quintilian. But again we will not stay; not only because the journey would take so long but because though many of these masters of rhetoric and oratory used examples from the theatre, none of them is specifically telling us about acting. About drama, about the three unities, yes—but not about acting. Quintilian in particular exclaims, 'For what can be less becoming to an orator than modulations that recall the stage?'

It is important to mention this, for it is true that Quintilian's *Institutes of Oratory* were used by the early theoreticians and Jesuit priests who were influential in the training of schoolboy and amateur actors in the seventeenth century, and it has been argued recently and with much persuasion, from this University,(22) that Elizabethan acting was founded on an understanding of rhetoric. That I am not going to attempt to disprove, but rather applaud Mr. Joseph's discretion in warning us that he would not necessarily advise us to 'attempt to reintroduce rhetorical delivery into our civilisation, either in our schools or in our theatres,' a warning which drew fire on his head from at least one quarter, if I remember, and doubtless disconcerted that section of our Shakespearean scholars who will not be happy till they have seen Shakespeare's plays restored to various facsimiles of the Old Globe Theatre, with penthouse, tiring-room, thatched roof, rushes, 'squeaking Cleopatras,' pseudo-Elizabethan phonetics and all. About this I have only two things to remark: that I only wish someone would do it, and do it fully and properly and get it all over, and also that I wonder, if Shakespeare were there to see it, whether he would not exclaim,

'Great heavens, you are not still doing it all like that, are you?'

It was not until 1747 that we have a work which completely broke with the previous oratorical school and which tasked itself to some kind of systematic discussion of the actor and the actor's art. *Le Comédien*, as it was called, is an important book, I think, and it certainly had much influence. The author's name was Remond de Sainte-Albine, a French journalist. As his anonymous translator observed in the English edition in 1750:

> You cannot be uninformed that Mons. *Sainte-Albine* some years ago gave laws to the *French* stage, which were founded on nature and reason, and therefore very unexceptionable: we know they were coolly received indeed by players, but the audiences thought so well of them, that they interested themselves to see many of them put in execution. . . .

I make no comment on the different receptions accorded it by players and public, but the book is indeed full of questions urgent to that time. To the subject of the oratorical manner in tragedy Sainte-Albine devotes a chapter headed:

'La tragédie demande-t-elle d'être déclamée?' (Should we declaim tragedy?') I quote from the English translation:

> Perhaps, among all the questions that have been or may be started upon the subject of the player's profession, there is no one about which the world is less agreed than this, 'Whether or not declamation be a proper manner of speaking for the performer in tragedy?' The occasion of all the diversity of opinions which we meet with on this head, however, rather arises from disputes about words than about things; and many who strenuously oppose the decisions of one another on the subject, only do it because they understand the terms *declamatory* and *declamation* in a different sense from one another.

About words rather than about things. . . . Ah, yes. . . .

Again, in a chapter headed:

du Jeu Naturel

The reason why we sometimes discover the study'd action of
the player, is not because he has been at the pains of studying it
beforehand, but because he has not study'd it enough: the last
touches of his application in this kind, should be those employ'd
to conceal that there ever was any labour bestow'd at all upon
what he is doing; and the rest, without this, always hurts instead of
pleasing us.

That may be simple, but it is acute.

On the relationship between sensibility and understanding,
he anticipates Talma's first two requisites of the actor: 'la sensibilité
extrême et l'intelligence extraordinaire'.

People who feel the most from reading a passionate speech in a
play, are not always those who understand it most perfectly; this
being the effect of sensibility, a peculiar quality of the mind, not
always, as already observed, proportioned to the understanding.
Either of these alone therefore will not do for the player; and as it
is plain he may possess one without the other, we are to acknowledge
the pretensions of that actor great indeed, who has both in such a
a degree that while the judgment regulates the sensibility, the
sensibility animates, enlivens, and inspires the understanding. (23)

The book is full of things of good sense. But Sainte-Albine
goes, or tries to go, deeper. If he does not entirely succeed, at
least for us today, it is only because our terms of psychology are
different and we hope more exact. He abandons the classic precepts
for the requirements of an actor—vocal and physical expression—
and since he knew that some great actors have lacked physical or
vocal means he proposes three others instead: *understanding*, 'for to
that he is to owe the proper use of all the rest'; *sensibility*, 'a disposition to be affected by the passions which plays are intended to
excite; and the third is *spirit or fire*. 'It is to this spirit and fire', he
says, 'that the representation owes its great air of reality. Understanding will make a player perceive properly, and sensibility will
make him do it feelingly. But all this may be done in reading the
passage; it is this fire and spirit that produce the living character,
and he who has judgment to regulate this, can never have too much
of it.'

As it has been put today in our more clinical jargon, the player must have 'sensory receptivity' and 'emotional activity'.

It is with terms like these that we begin to feel a change of temperature, of climate, of time and place. Where and when did we first hear terms such as these applied to the actor's art? Who was it introduced us to these, to the 'core' of a character, to 'units' and 'objectives' and 'super-objectives'? To the 'threshold of the unconscious'? I have sounded the name more than once yesterday and today. It is a startling name, and to mention it in our theatre, especially nowadays, is comparable to rattling an old, cracked thunder-sheet during someone else's lines. Nevertheless I shall have more, much more, to say of Stanislavski next week.

CHARLESTON

in *Thunder Rock*
(Ardrey)
Globe Theatre, 1940

Gordon Anthony
(Copyright :
The Gallery Studio)

KIPPS

in the film of that name
Gaumont-British
Studios, 1940

RAKITIN

in *A Month in the Country* (Turgenev)

St. James's Theatre, 1943

III

Instinct and Method—II

L AST week I suggested that to mention the name of Stanislavski in our theatre at this day and age is to invite suspicion. Even some six years ago I wrote of his book *An Actor Prepares*:(24)

> Quite a few actors have, I know, read it and have found it immensely stimulating. Other actors have read it, or partly read it, and find it fairly frustrating. Some others again say they have read it when what they mean is that they have always meant to read it. Some have read some of it and will frankly have none of it. Some would sooner be seen dead than reading it. For all I know some may even have died reading it. Very few have read it again.(25)

When those words were written the book had appeared in an American translation only some ten years before. What was not popular or fashionable in 1946 has become less than popular now. The whole legend of the great Russian actor-director-teacher, who died in 1938 is—*chez-nous*—decidedly *vieux jeu*.

The great ones—poets, painters, playwrights, philosophers, teachers—when they die, these great luminaries undergo a more awesome eclipse than do the lesser lights. The reaction against their work is swift and strong. This was once explained to me in these terms: when a great man is living among us the world feels a curious mixture of love and resentment towards him. The love we may understand. The resentment is what we unconsciously feel because his very greatness, while he is with us, reminds us of our own deficiencies. Our resentment in fact arises from fear. Once he has gone, after the first shock of loss that one who meant so much to us could ever leave us, we cannot help, however much we may have revered him, breathing a little more freely. He who was the measure of our own insignificance can now be measured with the other mighty and magnificent dead. Most of you are young enough not to have felt this change of heart towards Stanislavski, but I must confess that for some years now I have felt almost bored at the sound of his name and decidedly self-

49

conscious even in uttering it. However, I am ashamed to admit this, and in trying to make some plan for these talks, I quickly became aware that I could not bypass this landmark of the theatre with no more than a salute. For the work of Stanislavski is the only successful attempt which has ever been made to come to terms with the fundamentals of the actor's art.

Much has happened since he wrote his two greatest books some quarter of a century ago. Some of his own pupils have gone in different directions, though none, I think, has gone farther. Criticisms have been made, and I would even be prepared to embark on some myself if I were not certain that differences of language and inadequacies of translation did not add to my misunderstandings. It is worth remembering the passage I quoted last week from Sainte-Albine:

> The occasion of all the diversity of opinions which we meet with on this head, however, rather arises from disputes about words than about things.

It is so with many matters in the theatre.

The misunderstandings we may have about Stanislavski could probably be cleared up in a few minutes' conversation if one were able to converse with him. And at this moment, after re-reading many of his words and thinking what I would say to you about him, I can think of no one with whom I would more wish to have a talk.

The thing that comes to my mind now is something which I would not have thought of when I first read *An Actor Prepares* fourteen years ago. For then, though I was proud to think that I had already acted some forty different parts, I had only had some four years of strictly professional experience, and it has taken me all this time to see that there is a deep truth in the old actors' saying that it takes twenty years to make an actor.

That is not to say that an actor may not achieve artistic as well as professional success much earlier than that. All audiences have something in common with Kent in *King Lear*: they instantly recognise authority. And some actors have that authority—a result of character as well as experience—when still quite young. But it is rare.

Athuority itself, of course, is not enough. Nor, of course, are beauty of face, form, voice, nor personality nor individuality, though each of these in their turn have caused many a young man or young woman to believe themselves worthy to be paid for entering through the back door of a theatre rather than having to pay to enter through the front.

What takes so long for even the actor of exceptional gifts to discover is that essence of the art in himself which is style and that—in Henry James' words which I quoted last Thursday—'Style is expression, and expression the salt of life'.

It took Konstantin Sergeivich Stanislavski many years to find it. Like so many of us, he had glimpses of it, tantalising, ecstatically happy and damnably fugitive glimpses.

How, he wondered, could he see more?

Why must these moments be so fugitive?

The story of his stumbling efforts to discover the means to command the creative mood, the ever-elusive creative mood, is told in his autobiography, published when he was nearly sixty. A year or two later in Russia was published the book which contained what we call his 'system' or 'method'.

It is important to remember that the practical results of his findings, embodied in the work of the Moscow Art Theatre, were never seen outside Russia after the publication of his two books. It explains, to some extent, why the books, especially *An Actor Prepares*, encountered such a mixed reception. Another reason is that it is not generally understood that his Method is in effect 'only a conscious codification of ideas about acting which have always been the property of most good actors of all countries whether they knew it or not. Its basis is the work of the actor *with himself* in order to master "technical means for the creation of the creative mood, so that inspiration may appear oftener than is its wont" ...' [26] *An Actor's Work on Himself*, it has been said, [27] is a more accurate translation of the title.

Stanislavski had no desire to create inspiration by artificial means, for that would be impossible. He sought only to create by means of the will a favourable condition for inspiration to appear; 'that condition in the presence of which', as he put it, 'inspiration was most likely to descend into the actor's soul'.

It is not part of my purpose to go into any kind of detailed analysis of the method. That would involve at least several specialised lectures. On the other hand, I cannot assume, with what I know of the scope of your curriculum in this Drama Department, that you have all of you studied the system even in a theoretical manner, so I will try to give you a brief résumé of its purposes, while urging from the start that the only proper means of judging the effect of such a method is to put it into practice, which would take not less than three years and which, of course, cannot be done by the individual himself. It must also be borne in mind that the underlying idea of the method is to help the actor find the creative mood.

The basis of all the Stanislavski training was a physical one. 'As the painter has his canvas and his paints, so an actor has his body and his voice'. This is so obvious that it scarcely seems worth saying. But then a great deal of the method is obvious, as the teacher never ceased to point out. This physical training has now to some extent become a matter of course in all Drama schools. But we must remember that the thoroughness with which Stanislavski insisted that the physical training should be carried out was something quite new to schools of acting at that time. The importance of this thoroughness later led the state schools of Russia to insist that during the first year of a pupil's training he must not be allowed to utter a word on the stage. The great actors and actresses of that country continue their physical and vocal training throughout their lives, attending classes frequently, if not daily, as ballet dancers do. The opportunity for these classes is something which was offered to professional actors here at St. Denis' London Theatre Studio before the war. Since then nothing has taken its place. In New York some of the best young actors and actresses under Elia Kazan have formed the Actors' Studio where they practise physical movement and voice exercises and where a great store is set on improvisation.

The power of improvisation is something which is very much underrated in our professional theatre, where it is regarded as something a little bit amateurish or childish. It is not childish but

THE VENTRILOQUIST in the film *Dead of Night*, Ealing Studios, 1945

Cornell Capa

FRANK ELGIN in *Winter Journey* (Odets) with Googie Withers
St. James's Theatre, 1952

CHORUS in *Henry V*

Particam Pictures, Amsterdam

RICHARD II

in a solo performance of Shakespeare, Holland Festival, Amsterdam, 1951

rather child-like, and it is the faculty which an actor has to be like a child in his naïveté which helps him to avoid becoming a merely routine performer. It is paradoxical that in our commercial theatre, with its long runs, in the performance of which the actors are most in need of a stimulus to keep their imagination fresh and child-like, we should neglect the opportunity of exercising those qualities. Of course every really imaginative actor and actress has the power to improvise. We show it at rehearsals and also when things go wrong during the performance, such as when an entrance is missed or a prop is in the wrong place, and so on—contingencies which we meet with varying degrees of success.

I have had two notably interesting examples of the power of improvisation to affect the imagination, and through the imagination all the technical efficiency of the actor. In the last play in which I appeared, Clifford Odets' story of an actor who was the very opposite of the Stanislavski-trained actor (one of the reasons, by the way, why I accepted the part), the first act contains a scene in which this 'natural', this untrained actor is asked to give an audition, since he confesses to being a very bad reader, by means of an 'improvisation'. Odets, of course, supplies words for this improvisation, but during rehearsals, in order to get the imaginative feeling of what it is to do an improvisation, we decided to try to improvise the scene. The result of this trial was that we decided that we might never need to use the author's words at all, but that something would be gained by improvising afresh each night. So we did, and for eight months the two actors threw each other different lines. This was, of course, an exceptional case, but it had a most useful effect for me of making me wonder each night whether I would be able to succeed in the scene, which was exactly the feeling I needed before going on for the first scene of the play.

The other occasion was during the run of a play called *Uncle Harry*, which ran for about a year in London. I happened to be directing as well as playing in it. (A state of affairs in which the disadvantages outweigh the advantages, for if the director is playing a part in the play he is unable to get any objective view of either his own performance or other performances. There are other disadvantages as well, for the director occasionally finds himself torn between his feelings as a director and his concentration as an actor, and the other actors are liable to think that he is watching them with a critical, directorial eye even when he may not be doing so.) *Uncle Harry* had run several months, and the performances had lengthened by nearly twenty minutes since the opening night. It was also not, of course, as fresh as it had been in the first weeks. Now the chief interest of this is that it was extremely difficult to lay one's finger on the moments which were less spontaneous, since they seemed to the ear and eye almost exact replicas of what had been done all along. Nor particularly could one spot the cause for the longer playing time, for it was an accretion of minute causes.

I called a rehearsal and instead of re-rehearsing this or that scene, I put the actors' names, including my own, on bits of paper into a hat and as each name was drawn the actor was asked to go on the stage and improvise a scene based on his stage character but which would not occur in the play. The actors showed some apprehension and discomfiture, but were more or less cheerfully co-operative and they got through their improvisations with varying degrees of success.

All the characters in the play were what we roughly call 'character' parts, and I noticed that each actor during the long run had tended to alter the balance of the character, in so far as we all stressed more and more these aspects of the character which came most easily to us or were most successful with the audience. I told the other actors before we started how I had been told my own performance had altered, and asked them to consider whether this were true and whether similar things might not be true of their performances also. At the end of the improvisations I asked the company to be quite frank in judging whether each improvisation did not show the same change of emphasis as had happened during the run. With one or two exceptions we agreed that we had all changed, and that the improvisations showed it. In any case, the result was that that evening we gained not only an especially enthusiastic reception but regained all our lost time.

Of course in conditions such as operate at what might be called our two National theatres, the Memorial Theatre at Stratford-on-Avon and the Old Vic, especially when playing in real repertory with a change of play each night, the chances of growing stale are much less, and in any case, since for the most part one is rehearsing a new play in the day-time, the actors' imaginations are kept lively. So also is their vocal equipment.

But even if I have been rehearsing all day I would feel badly about going on for a heavy part at night if I had not taken physical exercise of some sort and also either gone to bed, which is preferable, or if there is no time for that, laid down on a sofa or, if necessary, the floor of the dressing-room. This habit of rest, by the way, was the practice of most of the old actors.

This brings us to the question of relaxation, which is Stanislavski's second main point. By relaxation he does not mean only exercise and rest, but what he calls work with the actor's personal psychology and the self-control of his nervous system. For the first requirement of acting is muscular freedom. I said in my first talk that I thought it preferable, especially in a heavy and tragic part, that the actor should feel some kind of subdued nerves every night. But, as I said then, quoting Jouvet, the good actor will know how to take advantage of these nerves. For the disciples of Stanislavski, the mastering of these nerves was achieved by a voluntary act of concentration which they called 'The Circle'. Each actor had to find for himself a means of creating an imaginary circle round him so that what happened outside that circle, although he might be obscurely aware of it, would not break his concentration. This should not mean, of course, that the actor is acting only for himself and ceasing to project. It may sound contradictory, and indeed it is hard to describe in scientific terms what this 'circle' is. It can only be said that once the actor has found it he will know what it means, and that he must endeavour to be able to find it each night. It is said that Nemirovich-Dantchenko, Stanislavski's partner in the founding of the Moscow Art Theatre, used to be able to find his circle of concentration by looking at his cuff links, and we hear of an actress who achieved it by closing her eyes for half a minute. These may sound absurd means of approach to what is an extraordinarily difficult state of mind to achieve. But in fact, to be paradoxical, what is so difficult to find must be found easily.

I remember years ago reading, in a book by Komisarjevsky,[28] that he recommended his pupils to try, before they went on to the stage, to feel very carefully the texture of some object—a piece of wood, the back of some canvas or the temperature of some metal object. At the time that I read this I was playing the leading part in T. S. Eliot's *The Family Reunion*, which requires that the hero on his first entrance shall meet his family, whom he has not seen for some time, and yet stare fixedly at the window where he is expecting to see the Eumenides which are haunting him.

The Family Reunion is, to say the least, a difficult play to perform, and it took me much time to learn the stresses of Eliot's verse let alone master them, and it was not until shortly before the opening that I made this extraordinarily difficult entrance in a way that I knew was right, in that it had the inner nervous tension without being melodramatic. But the harder I tried to recapture this emotion I had experienced at one rehearsal, the more difficult it became. The reason was that I was trying too hard. I religiously got myself ready for the entrance well ahead of time, kept as much as possible out of earshot of the actors playing the preceding scene, scrupulously followed Komisarjevsky's tip about examining the texture of some object. . . . The harder I tried the more completely I failed. The point of this, I think, is that it is not the looking at the cuff-links or the closing of the eyes or the feeling of the canvas which in themselves produce the relaxation which must precede the creative mood; but that having found it by some means or other with increasing frequency the actor is able to tie that feeling to a physical act, no matter what it may be, and that the reproduction of this physical act can automatically bring about the feeling. I say 'can'. It is a question of nothing less than faith. The touching of the object or the closing of the eyes becomes a sacred rite, and by means which I cannot put into analytical terms the act of faith offers a dispensation.

It is here that the actor who sinks his own personality and assumes not merely a strange make-up but the physical characteristics of another man has an advantage. For after the gropings in the dark, after some of the stresses and strains of rehearsals are over and a character has been found, the actor has only to achieve the walk or the set of the head or some other physical characteristic which he has found for the part, for the emotive impulse which he has already discovered in playing the part to come back to him. For such an actor the time at the make-up table, during which he watches himself slowly become Prospero or, in a shorter time, by a re-parting of his hair and composing his face to the point of world-weariness, feels that he is indeed Aubrey Tanqueray himself and not some character created by an author now dead, that time, long or short, is precious and magical. How preposterous and monotonous, by comparison, to this kind of actor, seem the long dozes in the make-up room at the film studio, where after what seems an eternity he is as a rule transformed into a tired edition of himself when young!

The next point to note in Stanislavski's method is the development of imagination and fantasy. These, he says, are the actor's two chief weapons. You may think there is no great difference between them, and here again we are to some extent baffled by mere words. What he meant by imagination was the actor's power to recreate impressions and emotions which he has previously received; by fantasy he meant the summoning up or simulation of feelings which the actor, who is no more omniscient than other people, cannot be expected to have felt. The second point is a tricky one. Obviously the actor who in life resists the emotion of love or is little acquainted with the emotion of jealousy will stand a poor chance if he comes to play Romeo or Othello. Who has not yet suffered to any degree will not communicate the feeling of suffering. A man lacking what we call a sense of the ludicrous is unlikely to make the audience laugh. But most of these feelings are common to the majority of mankind, and to have experienced them even in some degree may be sufficient.

It is at this point that I part company with the school of Walkley, against which, if you remember, I tilted earlier. The power of fantasy is the power to imagine what has never precisely happened to you. This of itself will not enable an actor to play a part, he cannot rely solely on fantasy. But the two powers of imagination and fantasy must be available to any actor, and supplementing each other they cover a large range of emotion. Though it is true that an actor is sometimes most successful when the part he is playing is based on a psychology analogous to his own, it is also true that with actors of a strong imagination and fantasy they can be surprisingly and sometimes overwhelmingly successful in roles with which they would appear to have no affinity. It is a sign of the truly creative actor, as it is also a sign of the creative playwright or novelist, that he will attempt to project characters which are often in strong contradiction to each other.(29) Life is so short and our understanding so limited that we very often judge each other by one set of characteristics. Even the simplest of us is some kind of psychologist, though a very faulty one. We forget to look, in other people, for the obverse of those characteristics, the virtues of their defects. We forget that virtues and defects can be equally strong. It is the privilege of the artist to be able to make use of both sides of the coin. 'Heads I win', he can say, 'tails you lose'. In so far as he is a creative artist, and only in so far, it is the actor's privilege also.

The next point to remember is what the author of the Method called, in translation, 'Offered circumstances'. This is simple enough to understand as an intellectual concept, for the 'circumstances' are those 'offered' by the author in his play. I would be tempted to leave it at that but that I know from experience how difficult it can sometimes be to persuade actors to accept these 'offered circumstances'. When I have directed a play I have sometimes asked an actor to ask himself why he thinks the author has written his particular part in the play. Absurd as it may seem, it is often very difficult to persuade actors to consider this point seriously. For the actor, especially with the economic pressure brought to bear on him in the conditions of a commercial theatre, finds it hard not to cling to the idea that the author has written the part especially for him. In ideal conditions perhaps every actor should go through the kind of play-writing course which you have here, and which had notable results under Professor George Pierce Baker in America. It is not so much a question of the actor 'knowing his place' in drama but of knowing his value. The faults of many actors derive ·from the fact that they are forced to consider their own aims and ambitions and to forget those of the author.

The fifth point is the question of naïveté, on which we have already touched. About this, Stanislavski wrote what for many people is his most baffling paragraph:

> I came to understand that creativeness begins from that moment when in the soul and imagination of the actor there appears the magical, creative IF. While only actual reality exists, only practical truth which a man naturally cannot but believe, creativeness has not yet begun. Then the creative IF appears, that is, the imagined truth which the actor can believe as sincerely and with greater enthusiasm than he believes practical truth, just as the child believes in the existence of its doll and of all life in it and around it. From the moment of the appearance of IF the actor passes from the plane of actual reality into the plane of another life, created and imagined by himself. Believing in this life, the actor can begin to create.[30]

Here is one of those moments to which I referred earlier where for a long time I found it difficult to bridge my misunderstanding with the author. For the proposition of the word 'If' is a purely intellectual proposition, and like many intellectual propositions, not easy to translate into action. Like the formation of 'The Circle' and *childish naïveté*, it is something which cannot be arrived at except by practical experience. Indeed it is really inseparable, this magic 'If', from both the actor's child-like and creative *naïveté* and his magic 'Circle'. But the truth is that it is really impossible to separate many of the aspects of the actor's art except in intellectual terms, and since the actor's art must always remain practical, intellectual terms must always remain unsatisfactory.

So it is with the question of 'contact' or, as it is expressed in the standard American translation, 'Communion'. Stanislavski says:

> Let it suffice now that you understand that *people always try to reach the living spirit of their object* and that they do not deal with noses or eyes or buttons the way some actors do on the stage.

Here again, it depends on how you look at it. For instance, it seems to me that in life we do not always try to find 'the living spirit of our object', but on the contrary, for the most part, try to project what might be called the living spirit of our subject, namely ourselves. Just as Proust said: 'In reality every reader, as he reads, is the reader of himself', so in life we interpret, unless in very exceptional moments of objectivity, other people through our own mood. Oddly and sadly enough, we *do* 'deal with noses, eyes and buttons', or shall we say in terms of things which are by no means 'the living spirit of our object'. But, as I said, here again a meaning has to be disentangled, and I think what Stanislavski means here is that the actor tends to externalise his intentions in order to make them clear to the audience, whereas in real life, in most situations among people whom we call civilised, the intentions are not overtly expressed. In my first talk I referred to the way that the best actors will 'listen' to each other, that it was a cliché of criticism to note how well an actor can 'listen'. Perhaps I gave too optimistic a picture of stage-practice. For only a few actors 'listen' all the time in the way that they should do, and every professional actor will be hurt if the director suggests to him that he is not really 'listening'. It is not only that some do not really 'listen' at all but only 'hear', but that there is the difference between listening in an artificial strained manner and listening as we listen in real life, which is to listen as spontaneously as we speak.

Then there is the difference between rhythm and tempo. Rhythm, which comes from within, and tempo, which is imposed from without. For a time Stanislavski attempted to subdue even rhythm to dictation and introduced a decimal system of 1 to 10 in which the normal tempo of life was 5 and which increased to 9 when a person imagined he was seeing a house on fire or when he was on the point of suicide and dropped to 1 when he was at the point of death. This marking of tempo was even included in the prompt copy for a time but Stanislavski later abandoned it as artificial. Rhythm cannot be dictated, whereas tempo can. It is worth noting that rhythm, when it can be achieved, is altogether more persuasive than tempo, pace or speed—but it is these three, which can be made more or less mechanical, which are more often praised.(31)

The final phase in the preparatory work on a role was to find what has variously been translated as the seed, the grain, the kernel or the core of the character, to which all the previous considerations are preparatory. This is followed by the 'aim' of the char-

HOTSPUR

in *Henry IV Part I*
Shakespeare Memorial
Theatre, Stratford-on-
Avon, 1951

Angus McBean

BARON TUSENBACH

in *The Three Sisters*
Queen's Theatre, 1938

(Copyright : The Gallery Studio) *Gordon Anthony*

Baron

SIR ANDREW AGUECHEEK

in *Twelfth Night*
Phoenix Theatre, 1938

ALEXEI

in *The White Guard*
(Bulgakov-Ackland)
Phoenix Theatre, 1938

Baron

acter and when the actor is conscious of this, all else is forgotten, for then the actor, as the character, can answer the question, 'What do I want and why?'

All these points have to be determined before the actor starts his work. During rehearsals we have to follow a number of other pointers scarcely less important. I will mention only the ones which are immediately intelligible, such as 'units' and 'objectives', a task whereby the actor breaks up his role into a number of small units governed by larger objectives; 'super-objectives' which are his aims for the entire part; 'the perspective of the role', and so on.

To find the 'aim' of the character Stanislavski asked his actors to consider not only the history of the character in the action of the play but his history before the play began, even when the author gives only the smallest suggestion as to what this previous life may have been. You will find examples of this in his book on his production of *Othello*([32]) where, in the discussion about the opening scene he suggests in a few paragraphs the previous life of Roderigo: 'What is the *past* which justifies the *present* of this scene?' he asks. 'Who is Roderigo?'

There follows a perfectly plausible summary of Roderigo's parentage, his financial and social position and a hypothetical description of how Roderigo first saw Desdemona, accompanied by her Nurse, stepping into a gondola; how he is struck by her beauty, which the Nurse, perceiving his attentions, persuades Desdemona to cover with her veil; how he follows them into the church where Desdemona is going to worship, and where by looks he makes her understand that he is interested in her; how when she returns to her gondola she finds it covered with flowers. And so on. How much value is there in what must seem to be a devious approach to Shakespeare's play?

I personally think, for reasons that I will give you next week, that the approach is not appropriate to the plays of Shakespeare, who is more impressionist than realist. But there can be no doubt that it works for certain kinds of plays, as many others beside myself have found from experience. But in either case it is, I think, work which the actor should do for himself and not let the director do for him. It may help the director to know what kind of past history the actor has worked out for himself, but for the director to suggest to the actors a whole new mass of detail which is not in the play, however relevant it may seem, only burdens the actors' imagination. The actor may not possess as clear a knowledge of both the play and its background as the director does, and he may need the director's help in sketching it all in. But the practical purpose of making these imaginary extensions to a play, extensions which cannot be communicated to the audience and have certainly no literary value, is to engage the imagination of the actor to the point where he feels he can identify himself with, or 'become' or 'live' the character. It would seem to be a wasteful process, and we can think of many fine performances which have been created without it. But nothing is wasteful in art provided that it adds even one jot to the total effect of what is being created.

Of course it is an expensive process in terms of man hours and the economics of the theatre. It is indeed a long cry from 'Learn yer words, dear, and then you'll *feel* it all right'. There are many who think that the Moscow Art Theatre, with its hushed corridors where no one was allowed to talk above a whisper and where the director, before beginning a rehearsal, greeted in person, with some formality, each one of his company, sounds a little too good to be true; smells, perhaps, too much of the museum. But here again, these customs had a practical purpose, and just as in our more happy-go-lucky English way a good director will try to establish a warm and friendly feeling among everybody working on the production, so Stanislavski's formalities served to remind everyone each day that one of his aims was to establish a certain dignity in his theatre. About the same period, Irving was also trying to achieve some dignity for the English stage. His methods at the Lyceum may have been different, but the intention was surely the same. As for the hushed corridors, when I think of the thousands of minutes and hours that are lost in the ordinary commercial theatre by the director having to yell at 'someone', 'somewhere' to keep quiet, there is no doubt which customs are more economical nor which atmosphere the actor would prefer.

I warned you of the dangers of a brief encounter with Stanislavski's method. It is not only that we have to 'Drink deep or taste not the Pierian spring', but that it is equally dangerous to try to put it into practice by ourselves. Though I said that his name is more or less tabu, it is evident from the number of books that continue to be published about him that there is a deep interest in the great Russian director. But to put it in as few words as possible, the main danger is that actors making their first acquaintance with his method mistake the truth of feeling, which he demanded, with *subjective* feeling, and I do not think that it is an overstatement to say that there are many talented young actors and actresses almost eating their hearts out on the stage but yet unable to communicate more than a fragment of their feelings to the audience. This is not quite the same thing as what is meant by —as has been said—'It is possible to act too well'. As Fanny Kemble wrote about one of her father's performances:

> I watched my father narrowly through his part tonight with great attention and some consequent fatigue, and the conclusion I have come to is this: that though his workmanship may be, and is, far finer *in the hand*, than that of any other artist I ever saw, yet its very minute accuracy and refinement renders it unfit for the frame in which it is exhibited. Whoever should paint a scene calculated for so large a space as a theatre, and destined to be viewed at the distance from which an audience beholds it, with the laborious finish and fine detail of a miniature, would commit a great error in judgment. Nor would he have the least right to complain, although the public should prefer the coarser, yet far more effective work of a painter, who, neglecting all refinement and niceness of execution, should merely paint with such full colouring, and breadth and boldness of touch, as to produce in the wide space he is called upon to fill, and upon the remote senses he appeals to, the *effect* of that which he intends to represent. Indeed, he is the better artist of the two, though probably not the most intellectual man.(33)

To be too intellectual is, of course, not the same as being too subjective but the effect of both excesses is the same: a failure to communicate. In the case of the young actors and actresses whose misinterpretation of Stanislavski's Method has led them to believe that they must 'do no more than they feel', it must be said that it is not altogether their fault but an inherent danger in a theory whose impetus was a reaction against all that was superficial and hollow in the theatre into which Stanislavski stumblingly, but with sincerity and simplicity and shining humility, found his way.

It was a reaction against this reaction which made Meyerhold, one of Stanislavski's pupils and leading actors, leave his master and establish his own theatre on radically different lines. This was at a time when the Russian proletariat was entering the theatre in large numbers for the first time, a public whose receptive powers were therefore not wedded to any theatrical convention. Meyerhold's success with the new audiences was phenomenal, and he dealt the Moscow Art Theatre a severe blow from the left.

Oddly enough, last Saturday, a correspondent to *The Times*(34), writing about the Romantic actors of his youth, made the point that our first acquaintance with theatrical conventions determines our subsequent reaction to others. He stated, in effect, that what we come to admire while still in the nursery maintains its pattern throughout our life. This is a familiar psychological dictum, but, I think, not true *in art* except in so far as it applies to more than ordinarily naïve people. If I am right, it can work the other way, and is another instance of the liberating power of art.

There is, I think, no historical precedent for Meyerhold and his new audience. In his new theatre for the new masses Meyerhold seemed to say, 'Let us turn our back on everything that the theatre of the old régime offered us'. The old régime, including the Moscow Art Theatre, asked its audience to forget that they were in a theatre and to imagine that they were living through the experience with the artist. Meyerhold postulated, and carried into practice with considerable success, the idea that the audience should always remember that it is in a theatre. In fact, he sought to establish a new convention which, of course, like so many new conventions, was in reality only a return to previous conventions, and Meyerhold could quote Molière and the Roman and Greek theatres to support him.

After what seems to me a rather curt nod to the author, whose 'truth', he said, 'had to be found', he worked to 'reveal that truth in theatrical form'. This form he called *jeu de théâtre* and around that he built his production. He pointed out that Molière was a

John
Vickers

THE CAPTAIN in *The Father* (Strindberg) with Jill Raymond
Duchess Theatre, 1949

John
Vickers

HARRY in *Uncle Harry* (Thomas Job) with Beatrix Lehmann
Garrick Theatre, 1944

ANDREW CROCKER-
HARRIS in the film
The Browning Version
Javelin Films, 1951

HAMLET

Old Vic Theatre
Company,
New Theatre, 1950

John Vickers

master of *jeux de théâtre*, that Molière would take a central idea and with great variety of invention, including comment, mockery, jokes, would do anything to put it over. (That this is not an accurate summary of Molière's intentions, I am aware.)

For instance, in a production of three short plays by Chehov Meyerhold announced to his company that he had found no less than 38 times when characters either faint or say they are going to faint, turn pale, clutch their hearts or call for a glass of water. He had asked his scenic director to produce a décor illustrating this central idea, which was to be something that resembled a large eye with a tear dropping out of it. In this, as in other Meyerhold productions, including his famous production of Gogol's *The Government Inspector*, Meyerhold would, we are told, use every line of the author's which served this central idea and either cut or re-write the rest.

Such, we are told, was Meyerhold's relation with his author, which of course I only derive through books or at second-hand, and you probably know as much if not more than I do about the 'constructivist' settings which Meyerhold persuaded his designers to use. These settings undoubtedly served his idea of what the author's idea was, and I expect it has been pointed out to you that in the use of these constructivist sets Meyerhold may have been something of an opportunist, since the materials out of which these settings were made were the only materials readily available in Russia at that time. It is possible also that he was an opportunist in other ways, and it has been suggested that in his idea of a Mass Theatre, though different in conception to the Mass Theatre of Max Reinhardt, he was, like Reinhardt, using the theatre to exalt his own ego. I will not pursue that idea beyond placing it in juxtaposition with his general theory about acting which consisted, to cut it unfairly short, of what he called 'bio-mechanics'. Just as the Art Theatre actor had said, 'I do this or I make this movement because my feelings tell me to do so', Meyerhold's bio-mechanical actor said, 'I make these movements because I know that when I make them what I want to do can most easily and directly be done'.

I think you will have gathered that I am not entirely uncritical in my reverence for what I know of Stanislavski and his Art Theatre, and I have to confess that I have been all too summary in my

5

description of Meyerhold and his methods. The reason I choose these two names is because *between* these two methods can be seen a method of acting and production which perhaps comes closer to 'Pure Theatre'. There can be almost no doubt that the Stanislavski method tended towards too great a subjectivity. There is some truth in the belief that it is mainly of use for psychological or realistic plays. Nevertheless there is a great deal of value which we can salvage from its only half-submerged wreck. There is also something of value in the bio-mechanical idea of Meyerhold.

In another Russian director, Vakhtangov, the two approaches seemed at least to converge. It was with Vakhtangov that the three leading spirits of the theatre, the author, the director and the actor, have come closest together. In my first talk I asked you to note that in the abdication of the star actor his place as autocratic head of state had been taken over by the director. Neither head is desirable, nor is it possible to envisage a usurpation by the author himself—unless of course, as in the case of Shakespeare and Molière, the author happens also to be an actor-director—in which case, if the author has eminent talents, it is eminently to be desired.

The reaction of Meyerhold against the Moscow Art Theatre is interesting chiefly because it is a struggle that is still going on. I said that time frequently lags to a standstill in the theatre, or seems to do so, for it is very interesting to see that the post-World War II theatre-movements in both France and Germany seem to be struggling to decide the very issue which Meyerhold tried to decide a number of years ago. In Germany there is the repatriated Bertold Brecht—an undoubted theatre genius if ever there was one—but still insisting on his ideas of Epic Theatre which he had adumbrated before the war, through which also the theatre is trying to establish a fresh convention in reaction against an old one. In Paris, also, that capital city of intellectualism, a theatre movement appeared a few years after the war, under the direction of an ex-Russian, Adamov, which significantly came to be known as 'Anti-Theatre'. The avant-garde are touchingly agreed that Adamov is making one of the most important contributions to the attempt at finding one's way in the modern drama. His stage methods, the avant-garde contends, will open up revolutionary perspectives'. But, as the critic from whom I have been quoting asks, 'Which perspective?' [35]

Just as Meyerhold was undoubtedly a genius of the theatre—at least in the Somerset Maugham definition of the word genius which is that a man should leave his unmistakable signature on his own work—so also is Bertold Brecht, and so Adamov has probably all that it takes to leave his own signature on his work in the theatre. But what is significant about Meyerhold and Adamov is their summary treatment of both author and actor. In effect their wish seems to be to reduce the actor to the role of Gordon Craig's *übermarionette* and the author to a cypher. Is it unfair to suppose that logically they would wish to banish the author from the theatre together with the actor? Could this possibly be true of Brecht who is, after all, his own author and a brilliant one also? This would seem to be still the struggle of our time in the theatre.

It is the battle of the word to survive.

The Theatre and the Word

I SPOKE last week of the battle of "the word" to survive. A melodramatic phrase, now I come to think of it, though it appears to be true that in some of the avant-garde theatres on the Continent a vigorous movement has been going on for a few years since the war to make pantomime (or *mime*) take a first place in dramatics, and that we in this country are already hearing echoes from what the previously quoted Franco-Danish critic has called those 'laboratories for dramatic experiment' where 'they are working at full steam on a kind of theatrical atom-splitting that is to renew the theatre fundamentally and to shatter the old prejudices about the dimensions of word, time and space.'[35] Whether our comparative aloofness from this kind of experiment is due to our native good-sense or our insularity I leave you to decide. But as actors we have to notice and take account of theatrical experiment. It is not only that public taste changes—how slowly on some levels and on others how fast!—but that we as actors can never rest on laurels, for if we do we are likely to be smothered by them. And just as I said that it is folly to speed the departure of a great spirit from our midst, it is also wise to remember that most of the greatest movements in the theatre have been hatched in similar 'dim laboratories.' One often notices, in the theatre, that those who turn their backs on what has happened after they first started forward have the appearance of going backward. The arteries of their talent harden, their reputation becomes rheumatic. Your business here at the moment is to grasp what has happened before you. Even the born genius must to some extent do that. Whatever your own originality may be, it is always well to keep an ear open to those 'dim laboratories' where, to quote the same critic again, 'people are ready to do anything without squinting for popularity or cash. The small theatres' (and we have one or two of them here) 'may be seen absorbed in their work as though it were a sacred cause . . . Nowhere do you get this feeling of pure idealism as you can in these cramped little theatres. Here, after all, is something you can still believe in—the art of the theatre.'

Whether this movement to establish *mime*, or physical action, and banish the word, which as I told you, has come to be known in Paris as Anti-Theatre, will ever take root here is perhaps doubtful, for it seems to me only an extension of expressionism, which we rejected swiftly. (As the lady in Emlyn Williams' play spoke of the birth of her sluttish daughter—'I took one look at her and I said, No!') But there are whispers of it in the air.

As it happens, we in England have just been attempting the opposite: the re-creation of a poetic drama. 'A powerful idea', it has been said, 'communicates some of its strength to him who challenges it.' Stanislavski's idea gave strength to Meyerhold, who strove very successfully for a time to attempt the opposite, or rather the obverse, of his master's idea. Brecht, in his manifesto on acting in his Epic Drama, also turns a theatrical table. The French movement of Anti-Theatre is perhaps a revulsion against the period of Giraudoux, Anouilh, Cocteau, for in the plays of those authors the word has dominance. So it has in the plays of T. S. Eliot and Christopher Fry.

Now it is true that some of the most significant moments in drama come when the actor scarcely speaks.

The poet and dramatist Paul Claudel recently remarked that he had noticed that the two moments in drama which had most moved him in his life occurred in works by dramatists for whom he had no high esteem. One of these is from Wagner's *Tannhäuser* (which, since it is a music-drama, we can scarcely count) and the other the sound, in the fifth act of Victor Hugo's *Hernani*, of the hero's horn blowing through the dark night.

Again, one of the most potent descriptions of significant moments in acting is contained in Gordon Craig's book on Irving. Craig has earlier mentioned what excitement it meant to a theatregoer of those days to be able to say, 'Tonight I am going to see Irving in *The Bells*'. When I was a small boy and my mother was acting in H. B. Irving's company at the old Savoy Theatre, I was allowed to watch *The Bells* from the flies—an unusual vantage point from which to see the turning of the women's Alsatian head-dresses and the strange pattern that this made from a flies-eye view. By general agreement, H. B. Irving, though a most remarkable actor in his own right, was not his father's equal. (It is a lasting regret of mine that I did not ever see Henry Irving's other son, Laurence Irving, who seems to have been much more of the true *comédien* than either his brother or his father, for my mother assures me that in two major parts she found him completely unrecognisable). I shall always remember peering over the fly-rail watching H. B. Irving execute the same business that is described in Craig's book. I also remember the strange silent scene in which Matthias is visited by the ghost of the Polish Jew, being, as I was then, peculiarly able to see not only the strange, dragging, bowed-kneed walk which H.B. inherited from his great father, whose every intonation and gesture he meticulously copied, but also the stage hands on the fly-rail throwing artifical snow on to the spectre of the Polish Jew standing glaring through the door, which opened with a sudden burst of wind. I also remember, as a young man, going to see Sir John Martin-Harvey, who was as much a disciple of the great Sir Henry as his elder son was, perform *The Bells à la Irving*. Though you might not think that any so careful a copy could be impressive, it was extremely so. Of course, the final touch of magic and inspiration which had come from the English creator of the role, and which were therefore his own, were lacking. But Martin-Harvey and H. B. Irving succeeded in fascinating their audiences, and these are very good examples of meticulous technique and loyalty to tradition.

Craig describes how, when the applause which greeted Irving on his entrance died away, the actor would cut it short by what Craig calls a sudden gesture of awakening, how he flung his cap and whip to right and left, began to take off his coat and muffler and how his wife and daughter came to help him. Then followed the process of getting rid of the coat and brushing off the snow as he stood by the door; how he worked his way, demonstrating all the physical effects of the extreme cold outside and the warmth of the house within (and how helpful it can be to the actor to remember and be able to show the physical temperature of the scene which he is playing!), and then began slowly to take off his boots and to put on and buckle his shoes. All this preceded a line from one of the other actors who casually mentioned that he did not remember such a night since what was called the Polish Jew's winter.

Matthias had murdered the Pole for his money, and at the mention of the words 'Polish Jew' this haunted man, who was at that moment buckling his second shoe, seemed to freeze. 'The crown of his head suddenly seemed to glitter and become frozen', as Craig says. And then the whole pace of this remarkable piece of physical acting changed and his audience could sense that his hands, which had hitherto been numb with cold, became numb with fear. Craig describes how his whole torso also seemed frozen and how he would draw himself up and straighten a little and lean against the back of the chair on which he was seated, and then held motionless, with fixed eyes that seemed 'fixed on us all', a pause of something like ten or twelve seconds. Now that is a long pause to hold, more especially at the beginning of a play, when the audience, however much they may have read about it, cannot be expected to know fully the reason for this terror. He then spoke his first line, which was, "Oh, you were talking of that, were you?" and, as I very well remember, from the performances of his son and Martin-Harvey, the peculiar thrill of the sound, far off, of the throbbing of sledge bells was heard.

I hope you can get from this description of a play which most of you can scarcely have seen the chief point of the scene from the actor's point of view: that Irving achieved this remarkable piece of suspense by the changes of physical tempo, which were then suddenly and frighteningly enforced by an off-stage effect. There can be no doubt that it was one of the great moments of acting, as all of you who have read Gordon Craig's book will be only too ready to believe.

Those of you who have not read it should certainly do so, for, only this side idolatry, it re-creates an impression of the power that Irving had over his sympathetic admirers, and one is only too ready to believe that it was a very remarkable power. Read also, for you will find them well-written as well as instructive, the memoirs of Joseph Jefferson (36). His great part, for which he was most famous, was that of Rip Van Winkle, who as a young man strayed up into the Catskill Mountains and remained asleep there for many years, returning to his home as a very aged man. Jefferson's description of how he gradually refined his 'business', how he avoided all suggestion of added realism but stuck always closely through many years to the imaginative core of the part, is illuminating, and perhaps nothing is more so than the very frequent question that was asked him as to how was his dog, Schneider. To many of his audiences it seemed a completely real dog, and they asked the question in all sincerity. Though Jefferson wisely never used a dog on the stage, the dog became as real to the audience as Rip Van Winkle himself.

These examples are not precisely what I meant by 'Pure Theatre', for they are Pure Theatre only in the sense of melodrama or 'hokum' raised by the power of the actor to the level of art. They call directly on the power of the actor, since they support him almost entirely by situation alone. Situation is a very powerful prop, but the business of drama is to move. The meaning of drama, by derivation, is to do, to act, to perform. The drama has also to move fast. The two hours' traffic of our stage has to get a move on.

But curiously enough the best way to get a move on in drama is not to move but to speak. That is not so odd as it sounds, for surely man first learned to speak in order to get things done, deeds which he could not accomplish without words.

It is here that we touch on the other meaning of 'Pure Theatre', the meaning I compared with 'pure painting' and 'pure music' at our first meeting. 'Pure Theatre', in this sense, compresses more happenings into less space than any other form of literature, while making them their most vivid. This is of direct concern to us as actors, for it is our job to communicate the size of what is happening as greatly as we can, the depth as deeply. Its swift urgency we must convey by being direct.

I do not know whether to you this seems woefully obvious or dismally complicated. Perhaps I can best illustrate it with a comparatively recent discovery which I have made concerning my own playing.

I said last week that I thought Stanislavski was mistaken to follow so psychological an approach to Shakespeare's characters, for if you remember I said that I considered Shakespeare more impressionist than realist in his presentation of character. The full truth of this was only lately made fully clear to me when playing Prospero in *The Tempest*, though when I emerged from that experience I realised that some others, including a few Shakespearian scholars, had come to something of the same conclusion.

Now I had played Prospero before as a much younger man, when my only approach to the character was the romantic one, based probably on the nineteenth-century critical attitude to *The Tempest*, which identifies Prospero and the drowning of his book with Shakespeare's farewell to his art and seeks to establish a character of remarkable sweetness and light. I would like to have seen how Stanislavski would have tried to reconcile Prospero with plausible psychological terms. I do not think it can be done. Prospero, in that immensely long expository opening scene, which might almost be taken as a test of the actor's power to arrest his audience's attention, is a man burdened with the problem of revenge. Not only everything he says and does but the whole atmosphere of the first scenes aim at wrong and revenge. He is presented to us as an almost god-like spirit of mercy—as when he released Ariel from the cloven pine— but a spirit of anger when he threatens both Ariel and Caliban with the punishments that may overtake them if they disobey him. Later, at the crux of the play, the voice of Ariel prompts him to question his motives of revenge, and in a very short space of time he who had for twelve years plotted the capture, amazement, confusion, madness, surrender and punishment of his enemies, is required not only to make a complete *volte-face*, prompted by a few words from Ariel, but what is most strange, *to continue in the outline of his plan while proposing a different dénouement.*

> *Ariel:* Your charm so strongly works 'em,
> That if you now beheld them, your affections
> Would become tender.
> *Prospero:* Dost thou think so, spirit?
> *Ariel:* Mine would, sir, were I human.
> *Prospero:* And mine shall.
> Hast thou, which art but air, a touch, a feeling
> Of their afflictions, and shall not myself,
> One of their kind, that relish all as sharply,
> Passion as they, be kindlier moved than thou art?

> Though with their high wrongs I am struck to the quick,
> Yet with my nobler reason 'gainst my fury
> Do I take part: the rarer action is
> In virtue than in vengeance: they being penitent,
> The sole drift of my purpose doth extend
> Not a frown further. Go release them, Ariel:
> My charms I'll break, their senses I'll restore,
> And they shall be themselves.

Ariel: I'll fetch them, sir.

Prospero then utters the great incantation beginning: 'Ye elves of hills, brooks, standing lakes, and groves. . . .' He entices his enemies into his magic circle, charges them, all unconscious, with their crimes and then, it is true, forgives them. He has lured his lesser enemies, Caliban, Trinculo and Stephano into a trap. He now exposes their shame in front of his greater enemies, whom he has already forgiven, and in the end dismisses them all and parts with his daughter while he, having previously, be it noted, 'required his dukedom' back again, proposes to set sail with them to Milan 'where . . . every third thought shall be my grave'.

Now it is all very well to say that Shakespeare intended Prospero's character to be a god-like one, intermixing the divine ingredients of wrath and compassion. And in such terms it is not difficult to understand the character when you see it or read it. But how do you act it? Do you say to yourself, 'I am a god'? for that is clearly very hard to carry out, especially in a character of such a tetchy disposition as Prospero. Or do you say to yourself, 'I am a human being who has suffered great wrongs, and so I am prepared to take the wrong means to set them right'? (An analogous case to the problem of Shylock?) Neither resolution is possible, I think, in practice, nor does the romantic solution recommend itself to us now, the solution which makes Prospero an epitome of divine forgiveness. I found—though I do not suggest for a moment that this is the only solution—that *for me* a clue to the character was contained in the two lines:

> And thence retire me to my Milan, where
> Every third thought shall be my grave.

These lines, which must come as a shock to audiences when the actor presents Prospero as a much younger man (on the silly, literal assumption that if he had a daughter of 14 he *need* not be so very old) provided me with the clue to some kind of theatrically effective Prospero in which I pictured him as a very old man who was uncertain that he could accomplish his task in time. The fact that he has a daughter of 14 does not worry any but the most literal-minded member of the audience, I think.

I must stress again that *for me* these two lines offered a solution. I do not for a moment suggest that Shakespeare had this idea uppermost in his mind, though it is true that earlier in the play Prospero has declared that he finds by his prescience that his

> ... zenith doth depend upon
> A most auspicious star, whose influence
> If now I court not, but omit, my fortunes
> Will ever after droop. ...

Nor would these lines necessarily offer any particular stimulus to another actor. To me, in that particular production, they did. Of course, these 'objectives' did not necessarily communicate themselves precisely to the audience, though in fairness to myself and the general idea I should record that the critics on the whole grasped the idea that I was playing Prospero as a tired old man who was desperately surprised that his magic ever worked.

It is said of the actress Maria Ouspenskaya that when a Hollywood director asked if a certain scene of farewell could not be played much faster she agreed to do so—while observing most forcibly that she did not feel that the character would be in a hurry at such a moment. But she instantly carried out the quicker change of tempo. The director asked her how, since she obviously did not agree with him, she accomplished this. She replied: 'I just said to myself: there is a taxi down below waiting for me—and it's ticking-up'.

This is not precisely 'truth of feeling', nor 'bio-mechanics'. But if you have got the idea, does it matter what we call it?

Shakespeare's use of 'impressionism' or some such term is better shown in characters such as Macbeth or Marc Antony. In the first act Macbeth is what the script writers would call 'heavily planted' as a 'noble' character, yet in his very first soliloquy after his meeting

with the witches he mentions the thought of murder as a means to
gain his end. Antony is described as noble no less than eight times
in the play, but his nobility and Cleopatra's sex-appeal are for the
most part left for other characters to illustrate.

These examples from Shakespeare are convenient, not only
because I know them from personal experience but because it can
be assumed that you are acquainted with the texts. You will also
know that Shakespeare employed what the Shakespearean scholars
called 'double-time'—as he did for instance, in *The Merchant of
Venice*—compressing the action of what is clearly three months
into what is seemingly three days. In the same way, actors can use,
not only in Shakespeare's plays but, I suggest, in others, a double-
psychology or double-plausibility, depending from line to line on
the plausibility of human behaviour but yet in a scene or perhaps
in a moment cementing a process that in real life might take days
or months. There is an example of this in the character of Vera in
Turgenev's *A Month in the Country* where the occurrences of Act 4
transform her, a young girl, into a woman overnight. 'Today,'
she announces 'I am a woman'. The actress who plays the part
must really convince the audience that she has, as it were, become
a woman. Logically or realistically we might resent this. In a
novel the process might be accomplished by a long paragraph; in
the theatre it has to be accomplished in a line, and by acting. It is
'Pure Theatre'.

You will see that what I am suggesting is that for acting Shakespeare an approach must be found which makes use not only of the
Stanislavski method—which would seem to be psychological
plausibility but whose main objective, I nevertheless will remind
you, is to *find the creative mood*—but also of something similar to
Meyerhold's 'bio-mechanics': the precept that 'if I do this and this
so and so will be the effect'.

Irving, when he rehearsed at home, watched himself in a glass,
as did Thomas Betterton two hundred years before him. Whether
they knew it or not, they were both practising 'bio-mechanics'.
Indeed in the 'Life' of Thomas Betterton you will find a long quotation from a learned Jesuit describing the various actions of the hands,

motions of the head, expressions of the eyes and mouth and what these all signify. It is not so surprising that they should mean much the same today.

A certain element of the 'bio-mechanical' is not only permissible but helpful. It becomes dangerous the moment the audience can spot what is happening and senses the artificial. You must to some extent, as the old actors said, 'wrap it up'. (Nevertheless, we must know what is in the parcel.) The 'unbroken line' of thought and feeling which Stanislavski demanded can be achieved, though it is seldom achieved throughout a performance, however much the Stanislavskidolator insists that it may be. Lotte Lehmann, whose performance of The Marschallin in *Rosenkavalier* was as notable for its acting as its singing, confessed, while at the height of her career, that she had only given four performances in her life which totally satisfied her. The case of a singer who is called upon to play a leading part which demands great sensitivity as well as authority in its performances is a rare one, it is true, for to the problems of the actor are added the problems of the singer. Those who ever saw Lotte Lehmann in the part of The Marschallin will appreciate the size of the difficulties—difficulties which this great artist hid with such enormous art.

It is necessary for the young and ambitious actor to have a sense of the size of his life's task, to feel what Yeats called 'the fascination of what's difficult'. He must say to himself quite early on, 'What kind of actor do I wish to be?' He must think in terms of the size of his ambition, strengthen and enlarge every part of his equipment, his physical and vocal powers, his knowledge of dramatic literature and, indeed, his knowledge of all the arts. 'But more important than these'—I seem to hear someone exclaim—'is to live'. The ideal programme is indeed so vast that it would scarcely seem to give him any time for coming to terms with real life. Fortunately life has a way of taking human beings in hand. Ellen Terry retired from the stage in her early twenties, when she was already a successful actress, for several years in order to rear her young family. Many a young actor and actress whose career was just beginning to take shape in 1939 had that career abruptly and cruelly arrested. On returning to the theatre they might have had every excuse to feel that the war years were wasted and that they had to begin all over again. But it is very noticeable that in most cases they came out of the services much better actors and actresses than when they went in.

Much of the savour of life comes from contrast, and an enforced contrast in our ways of life helps sometimes to give us a perspective. It is all very well to say, as I have just said, that the actor should ask himself, 'What kind of actor do I wish to be?' but what we wish and what we achieve are never quite the same. After many years of working as an actor, teacher, director, author, Jacques Copeau was offered the post of administrator of the Comédie-Française. He wrote to Granville-Barker asking Barker's advice as to whether he should accept the post. I quote you two long extracts from Barker's letter in reply:

> You are good enough to ask me whether I think you should accept the directorship of the Comédie-Française if it is offered to you. Yes, I do.
>
> Upon principle, you should. André Maurois, that most apt and valued interpreter between my country and yours, has lately quoted with approval one of the minor watchwords of the British Army: Never ask for a job, never refuse one. You have not asked for this. But if you see any reasonable chance of putting the principles you stand for into practice at the Comédie, it is an opportunity and a duty you cannot refuse. Make what conditions you must, but the fewer the better.
>
> Some people may wonder that you make any question about it. How refuse such a prize? But I know very well why you stand in doubt. You did not first sink your literary career in the quixotic enterprise of the Vieux Colombier, nor leave that rather than surrender it to mere profit-making and go out into the wilderness (even the blossoming wilderness of the Côte d'Or) and begin again from the beginning, to be tempted at this time of day by the externals of success. You are asking yourself whether the straight and logical road you have followed (those who think it other cannot have thought about the matter at all) really leads you to the corner of the rue de Richelieu. As you ask me also, I must tell you why I think it does.
>
> . . . You went to Pernand, did you not, because you felt you were not on firm enough ground at the Vieux Colombier. You wanted to 'kiss the soil' and regain strength. Well, you construct and

perform, you and your actors, one quite primitive play, very simple, very genuine; that is kissing the soil to some advantage. The next day you gave us Molière. It does not become a mere Englishman to speak on the subject; but if that was not a truly traditional performance, with all the spirit and the strength of Molière conserved, and all the dead redundancies of so-called tradition cut away, then I never saw or imagined such a thing. Do you see now why I think you are heading—and always have been—towards the rue de Richelieu?

I wrote to you afterwards, you may remember, begging you to spend no more time kissing the earth or laying foundations but to go ahead with your building; that is to say, with the interpreting of one good play after another, letting the art of one beget the better art of the next. For—to keep to the apter metaphor—once the strain is sound, that is how good art does naturally increase, and after painful years of gestation it will suddenly come to amazing fertility and flower in a hundred unexpected ways. Moreover, all the virtue goes out of a simplicity that is guarded too carefully and too long, and it becomes an affectation of the barrenest sort. Besides, you yourself it seemed to me had by this completed a remarkable apprenticeship, begun when you bound yourself twenty years ago to the single-minded service of your art. (37)

I make no apology for quoting at such length. I will even repeat a line or two of this remarkable letter: 'Once the strain is sound, that is how good art does naturally increase, and after painful years of gestation it will suddenly come to fertility and flower in a hundred unexpected ways.'

When I said in my first talk that the desire to act must become an obsession, I did not mean that it should become a total obsession. Quite simply it means that if you are going to produce the best work of which you are capable, that work will, sooner or later, take first place in your mind. The young actor, having become aware of his ambition in wider terms than the vague general ambition of personal success, must prepare himself for the day when the chance comes of achieving that ambition, for by these means his constant dedication to his purpose will bring that ambition into sight. It is no good his wishing that one day—any day, tomorrow, perhaps—he will be given the chance to play such and such a part. It is rather that all his labours, together with his attitude towards his work and of course his talent, will one day bring that chance within range. It is not a matter of luck, though of course chance takes a hand in the theatre as in every other human activity. The actor will, if he wishes it and works for it enough, attract towards himself the circumstances and events he deserves. He must create his own luck.

This is easy to say, but it requires a golden patience as well as iron courage and determination. Granted these three qualities, the difficulties of his art, like the difficulties of life, give him an added strength.

Our present age presents its own set of difficulties, both in life and in that part of it which is the acting profession. All in all these are probably no worse than the difficulties of previous ages. But the modern actor, with his inheritance of the well-made naturalistic play, together with the example before his eyes of the cinema where he can see what appear to be brilliant performances by people who in the ordinary sense of the word are not actors at all, receives little or no stimulus to practise what is difficult. Among the thousands of plays that are written and the few hundred that are performed each year there are very few which offer parts to the modern actor in which he can stretch his powers. That is one of the reasons why our actors turn and have always turned to Shakespeare. It is not, as is sometimes suggested, the actor's wish for a big fat role nor the management's desire to avoid the author's royalties that has prompted so many Shakespearean revivals, but rather the natural desire of the actor who has begun to feel his strength to try it with mighty opposites. Once the actor has played some of these great parts the 'run-of-the-mill' modern drama seldom stirs his ambitions.

Last week when we reconsidered the seven or eight main points of the Stanislavski system, we touched on all the main requirements of the actor. These have been repeated and repeated in different form and in different words by everyone who has ever tried to formulate a conception of what the actor needs: physical equipment, voice, naïveté, imagination, and so on. But so often the actor who excels in certain aspects of his craft is tempted to rely more and more

MACHEATH

in *The Beggar's Opera*
with Audrey Mildmay
Haymarket Theatre,
1940

Angus McBean

PORTRAIT

Douglas Glass, 1953

Reproduced by permission of *The Sunday Times*

F. T. Holte

SHYLOCK

in *The Merchant of Venice*
Shakespeare Memorial Theatre, Stratford-on-Avon, 1953

on what comes most easily to him. A well-placed, resonant and pleasing voice has been the downfall of many. It can be almost as fatal as an exquisite face and a beautiful body. When the actor has gained some mastery of the essential qualifications, his difficulties have only just begun. He must in the first place strengthen his mastery of all these things so that in each of them he can feel a great reserve of power and then he must, by his intelligence or taste, know how not to use these powers to the full. He must know, in fact, what to leave out. (Not at all the same thing, it must be noted, as 'underplaying'.) Cicero, describing the delivery of the actor Roscius, tells us how in certain speeches the actor would carefully prepare his big effects by deliberately sacrificing previous effects. Delsarte, the great French teacher among whose pupils was Rachel, wrote:

> Without abnegation, no truth for the artist . . . we must often leave people in ignorance of our own good qualities.

William Poel wrote in a letter to the *Saturday Review*:

> As with all the other arts, so it is with good acting, its excellence lies in restraint and in knowing what to surrender. If elocution is to imitate nature, a dozen or more words must be sacrificed so that one word may predominate and thus give the keynote to the tune of the whole sentence. In this way only can the sound be made to echo the sense. But the last thing, apparently, the actor cares to do is to give up making every word tell. Redundancy of emphasis is his besetting sin, especially in the speaking of verse.
>
> Thus Shakespeare, without elaborate scenic accessories, is un-attractive on our stage, because our actors rarely bring intelligence to what they are saying. . . . Only recently at a West End theatre, a leading actor of repute spoke the following words of *Macbeth* thus:
>
> 'or *why*
> *Upon* this BLASTED *heath* you stop *our way*
> With *such* prophetic *greetings?*'
>
> . . . The speech as spoken conveyed no sense to the listener . . . There are three words only that need inflecting in the sentence ('why', 'stop' and 'prophetic') with the emphasis either on 'stop'

6

or 'prophetic'. If these three words are rapped out and heard distinctly, the listener knows what the rest of the sentence means, and the whole can be said very quickly. Of course to speak rapidly on the stage and clearly at the same time requires not only a flexible voice but severe training in exercises. . . . Compared to the French or the Germans the English are bad listeners when they get inside a theatre. (38)

Part of Poel's ambition in putting Shakespeare back into an Elizabethan form was that he wished to prove that the plays could indeed occupy 'two hours traffic of our stage,' which, with selection of emphasis and with the verse spoken 'trippingly on the tongue,' he proved was more or less attainable. Poel's lesson was never thoroughly learned except by a few of his notable disciples and it is in danger of being forgotten. At a recent production of the play in which Shakespeare refers to the 'two hours' traffic of our stage' —despite the fact that there was no change of scenery and only one interval and that one major scene was cut—I noted that it lasted over three hours and a quarter. The actors—or at least some of them—seemed so intent on thinking every line and almost every phrase and occasionally even single words, that one sometimes lost the total sense of what they were saying. We actors frequently under-estimate the quickness of an audience's mind.

Recently, at a matinée celebrating the centenary of William Poel's birth, Sir Lewis Casson gave a vivid demonstration of how Poel would teach his actors to inflect their speech. This, he explained, was necessary not only to give variety of tone and to guide the ear towards the sense of a speech, but because in an auditorium of any size, however good the acoustics may be, if the voice stays too long on one tone or a semitone above or below, the sound is apt to become confused and we cannot hear what is being said. This variety of inflection—which does not come very easily to many English people—demands an extraordinary range and variety of tone. Rossi, with his demand for 'Voice', 'voice' and then 'voice', was not alone in thinking that voice is the chief requirement of the actor. I would like to read you a passage about a fictional actress. Marcel Proust called her 'Berma' and we have no difficulty in seeing in her a portrait of Sarah Bernhardt—and for once I think we are allowed to assume that at this moment the author meant us to see a living person through a fictional character.

Berma's voice, in which not one atom of lifeless matter refractory to the mind remained undissolved, did not allow any sign to be discernible around it of that overflow of tears which one could feel, because they had not been able to absorb it in themselves, trickling over the marble voice of Aricie or Ismene, but had been brought to an exquisite perfection in each of its tiniest cells like the instrument of a master violinist, in whom one means, when one says that his music has a fine sound, to praise not a physical peculiarity but a superiority of soul; and, as in the classical landscape where in the place of a vanished nymph there is an inanimate waterspring, a clear and concrete intention had been transformed into a certain quality of tone, strangely, appropriately, coldly limpid. Berma's arms, which the lines themselves, by the same dynamic force that made the words issue from her lips, seemed to raise on to her bosom like leaves disturbed by a gush of water; her attitude, on the stage, which she had gradually built up, which she was to modify yet further, and which was based upon reasonings of a different profundity from those of which traces might be seen in the gestures of her fellow-actors, but of reasonings that had lost their original deliberation, and had melted into a sort of radiance in which they sent throbbing, round the person of the heroine, elements rich and complex, but which the fascinated spectator took not as an artistic triumph but as a natural gift; those white veils themselves, which, tenuous and clinging, seemed to be of a living substance and to have been woven by the suffering, half-pagan, half-Jansenist, around which they drew close like a frail, shrinking chrysalis; all of them, voice, attitude, gestures, veils, were nothing more, round this embodiment of an idea, which a line of poetry is . . . than additional envelopes which instead of concealing showed up in greater splendour the soul that had assimilated them to itself and had spread itself through them, than layers of different substances, grown translucent, the interpolation of which has the effect only of causing a richer refraction of the imprisoned, central ray that pierces through them, and of making more extensive, more precious and more fair the matter purified by fire in which it is enshrined. So Berma's interpretation was, around Racine's work, a second work, quickened also by the breath of genius.[39]

This recreates not only some of the pity and terror which great playing can excite but gives a picture of how the actor can be a creative artist in his own right while still remaining faithful to the author. It makes us more than ever convinced that of all the qualifications of the actor, voice should come first. The voice, beyond all other things, convinces us of truth. A phrase in vogue just now is 'The moment of truth'. It derives, we are told, from the Bull-ring and it has come to mean that moment when what we do or say has the stamp of inevitability, something which cannot be forced or faked. It is worth noting that a much older phrase is 'the ring of truth'.

When I was an undergraduate I remember the philosopher Lowes Dickinson, perhaps the most revered as well as the most loved of the Grand Old Men of Cambridge, sitting with his skull-cap on, puffing at his pipe and saying gently, though with impressive pauses: 'The older I get . . . the more I think—that it isn't what people say that matters—it's . . . the way they say it'. That is a simple and profound truth, however unpopular it may be with people whose minds are moulded by accepted opinion or by dogma.

But the ring of truth in life, you will say, has nothing to do with voice-production, elocution, diction. That is true; the truth comes from within, from the mind and heart. But to express the truths of the theatre we must have a voice that will carry every sound, every nuance, to the farthest corner of the house. In the cinema the lens can be close to our faces and register a slight narrowing of the eye or a twitch of some special muscle. The microphone hangs over our heads.

The eye can also be deceptive. The ear is not so easily deceived. We must all of us have noticed that the totally blind usually seem more happy and trusting than the deaf, those terrible unfortunates who live in a world of silence. Though we may disagree about terms and phrases, the word gives the voice meaning. and the voice gives the word its ring of truth. To put this in more practical terms, listen, as we all have to do sometimes nowadays, to the average radio-play from the next room or from a neighbour's house. Or, if you are an actor, shut your eyes at a rehearsal and see which voice *compels* you to listen to it. Whatever compels you to listen is telling, after its fashion, the truth.

    ★   ★   ★   ★   ★   ★   ★

'The Actor's Ways and Means.' . . . I warned you when I started that I would not attempt to build up any new theory of the actor's values or responsibilities. I have on my desk a large pile of notes and references which I have been unable to assimilate. I thought of these this afternoon as I walked down here and saw, in large letters outside the Chapel by the Victoria Rooms, a most startling and memorable misquotation; the 'Thought for the Week':

"THERE IS A DIVINITY ROUGH-HEWS OUR ENDS,
SHAPE THEM HOW WE WILL."

I am grateful for the chance which your University has given me to try to put into words, however rough-hewn, something of what I think about the different aspects of the actor's art. I think that perhaps I may have learned something by the attempt. I am satisfied if I have given you any kind of stimulus one way or another. I am aware that I have not achieved a synthesis but I knew I would not do so. This is an interim statement and the account does not balance.

Of one thing, however, I have become certain and I can best express it in the words of Granville-Barker to Jacques Copeau in the letter from which I quoted earlier this afternoon: *The art of the theatre is the art of acting, first, last and all the time.* Granville-Barker was a playwright as well as actor and director. He wrote those words some years ago. I do not think he would ever have wanted to change them.

The actor's position today is an anomalous one. It will always be so. As La Bruyère said: 'The actor was disreputable in the opinion of the Greeks', and he went on to add: 'We ourselves esteem them as the Romans did and live with them as the Greeks'. I cannot see that the state of things has altered. Does it greatly matter? No. For the real actor the only place where he is truly at home is on the stage—whatever kind of stage it may be. The true actor is in fact one who is 'à l'étroit chez-lui'; in the spiritual sense, he is only at home when he is not himself. To be at his real home he will tear himself away from loved ones, lover, life itself. 'I am grateful,' said Joseph Jefferson in an interview after his retirement, 'for this life of illuminated emotion'.

In another interview Dame Madge Kendal is reported to have said that her profession was not a subject she was ever anxious to speak about. Here, perhaps, we cannot quite believe her, for she managed to speak quite a lot about it. But when she qualified the previous statement by adding that nevertheless she would only be silent about it when the worms were in her heart we know that she was speaking the truth.

Notes

(1) 'How to Criticise a Novel,' by David Daiches (*The Listener*, September 18th, 1952).

(2) Sir Desmond MacCarthy. *The Sunday Times*, March 11th, 1951.

(3) *The Unholy Trade*, by Richard Findlater. (Gollancz, 1952).

(4) However, a play by Mr. Greene has now been sighted off the coast of Sweden.

(5) *Giraudoux par lui-même*. (Editions du Seuil, Paris, 1952).

(6) *Réflexions du Comédien*, by Louis Jouvet (Editions de la Nouvelle Revue Critique, 1938).

(7) *The Times*, April 22nd, 1924.

(8) *The Scenic Art*, by Henry James. (Rupert Hart-Davis, 1949). From the Essay on Coquelin reprinted from *Constant Coquelin, Art and the Actor*, translated by Abby Landgon Alger. Copyright 1915 by Dramatic Museum of Columbia University.

(9) If it were otherwise, would not Henry James' and Bernard Shaw's condemnations of Irving rate lower than the praises of the same performances written by Archer and Walkley? It is the custom to say that Shaw and James were prejudiced on the subject of Irving. Perhaps so, yet no one accuses them of much prejudice elsewhere. I cannot put my point more clearly, nor I think, more fairly than if I say that I have been astonished to find a critic praising me for something that never entered my head.

(10) See Mr. Findlater's book, which I mentioned earlier, where is to be found one of the latest and perhaps the fullest guides to the place.

(11) Stanislavski was, of course, an outspoken opponent of the star system. But we must remember that the star system which he opposed was the bad old star system of the nineteenth century. We may wonder whether he would have used quite the same harsh terms about the best of our companies today, where a peaceful revolution has taken place and where for the most part 'star' actors and actresses

seldom behave as they are still commonly supposed to do. I say this not in order to flatter some of my contemporaries but because, due to the time-lag of opinion which operates among the theatre public as strongly as it operates elsewhere, it is still commonly supposed that actors, especially leading-actors, spend much of their time in pursuing ridiculous quarrels accompanied by much extravagance of behaviour. This is sometimes encouraged by certain sections of the press who know that nothing sells the papers better than accounts of devilry, distress and disaster. The late James Agate, in a list of what he called the prerequisites of the great actor, closed with: 'a ruthless determination to suppress every promising younger rival.' Books are still written in which it is automatically assumed that the word 'star' is synonymous with every kind of selfish behaviour. 'None of that "star nonsense" '—we have heard the cry even from those who betray a keen anxiety to have their names in lights. One must speak only as one finds, and in my experience the best actors and actresses of our theatre do not behave in this outrageous way. The history of the theatre can hardly ever have seen a gesture more generous than that of a great actor producing a younger man in one of his own great roles. Yet this is what Gielgud did when he directed *Richard II* with Paul Scofield in the name part, a part he is still perfectly capable of playing himself. No, it is mainly a few actors in whom ambition is raging and unfulfilled who will misuse other actors, the author, the play even, to advance themselves.

(¹²)   So strongly did Shaw feel about this—and I am sure, so rightly— that in his own plays he was not only adamant that no word should be changed or cut be made without his permission, but he even contrived to write his plays so that they were what we call 'actor-proof'. It is very difficult to alter Shaw's intentions in performance (though I hasten to add this does not mean they are easy to perform.)

(¹³)   It is to the credit of Reinhardt's genius that so much of this detail plotted in advance did 'work', and worked very effectively, especially when he could employ a cast of brilliant German actors. What happened when, in later years, he tried to impose the same kind of pattern on inferior or amateur actors was another matter. It would not be fair to judge him by the O.U.D.S. production nor the Hollywood film of *A Midsummer Night's Dream*.

(¹⁴)   *Henry Irving*, by Laurence Irving (Faber & Faber, 1951).

(15) *Antony and Cleopatra* (The Folio Society, 1951).

(16) *Acting and Behaving*, by Alexander Knox. (Los Angeles: *Hollywood Quarterly*, Vol. I, No. 3, April, 1946).

(17) T. C. Worsley, *The New Statesman*, July 26th, 1952.

(18) *Acting*, by Robert Speaight (Cassell & Co., 1939).

(19) *Time Was*: by Graham Robertson (Hamish Hamilton, 1931).

(20) *The Art of the Actor*, by C. Coquelin. Translated by Elsie Fogerty (George Allen & Unwin, 1932).

(21) Lee Strasberg: Introduction to *Acting: a handbook on the Stanislavski Method.* (C. Lear. New York, 1947).

(22) *Elizabethan Acting*, by B. L. Joseph. (Oxford University Press, 1950).

(23) *The Actor:* A Treatise of the Art of Playing.

(24) *An Actor Prepares*, by Konstantin Stanislavski. Translated by Elizabeth Reynolds Hapgood (*Theatre Arts*, New York, 1936).

(25) *New Theatre*, reprinted in *Actors on Acting.* (Crown Publications New York 1949)

(26) *Moscow Rehearsals*, by Norris Houghton (George Allen & Unwin, Ltd. 1936)

(27) *Stanislavski on the Art of the Stage*: David Magarshack. (Faber & Faber Ltd., 1950).

(28) *Myself and the Theatre*: Theodore Komisarjevsky. (William Heinemann, 1929).

(29) It was Gogol who said that all the characters in *Dead Souls* were in fact dark sides of his own nature and that he wished, by expressing them, to annihilate them in himself.

(30) *My Life in Art*: Konstantin Stanislavski. Translated by J. J. Robbins (Geoffrey Bles, 1924).

(31) It is also notable that personality acting—or 'straight' acting—can 'get away' with inconsistencies, contradictions in characterisation much more than the other kind of acting, whatever name we give it.

(32) *Stanislavski produces Othello*: Translated by Dr. Helen Nowak (Geoffrey Bles, 1948).

(33)　Fanny Kemble's Journal.

(34)　*The Times*, Saturday, November 15th, 1952.

(35)　Anne Chaplin-Hansen, *Teatereksperimenter og Anti-Teater.*
(Beslingske Aftenavis, Copenhagen 28, August 1952).
Translated by R. P. Keigwin.

(36)　*"Rip Van Winkle": The Autobiography of Joseph Jefferson.* (Reinhardt
& Evans, 1949).

(37)　*Theatre Arts Anthology:* (Theatre Arts Books, Robert M. MacGregor,
New York).　Reproduced by the permission of the Executors of
the late Harley Granville-Barker.

(38)　*The Saturday Review:* July 31st, 1909.　I am grateful to Mr. Robert
Speaight for drawing my attention to this letter by William Poel
and for allowing me to read a chapter of his forthcoming book
William Poel and the Elizabethan Revival. (Heinemann).

(39)　*Remembrance of Things Past:* (Vol. 5).　Marcel Proust.　Translated
by C. K. Scott Moncrieff.　(Chatto & Windus, 1941).